Wars of Kings

Wars of Kings

Edward Moore

Columbus, Ohio

Wars of Kings

Published by Gatekeeper Press
2167 Stringtown Rd, Suite 109
Columbus, OH 43123-2989
www.GatekeeperPress.com

ISBN (paperback): 9781662909337

This book contains writings spanning from more than 4,000 years ago and continuing through the present time. It is presented as the history of humanity's existence, in seven periods of time measured in the progression of technology.

Time Period 1: *Innocence*

The ancient records tell us mankind was created by God. I know that this assertion will be disputed by many, but in reality, the many can offer no physical proof of their view. The truth is the Earth itself contains ample proofs in records we can show. For example, fish live in water, producing after their kind, while man is produced from the dust of the Earth. Every human body contains all elements found in Earth. Another proof is that animals do not grow in intelligence ever to the level of man, while man's intellect *never stops growing!* We now present man's first technology on Earth.

Adam and Eve existed from the fruit of the Earth, and Adam's first technical achievement was tilling the Earth, then harvesting its produce; even this technology has been vastly increased by technology advancement during our time period. The *political level of man's life* went backward into the first MURDER of a human; it was the murderer's, Cain's, own brother. This technology has increased in magnitude and efficiency almost beyond expression. The political community of the days of Noah grew in size and evil so that the record says, "The thoughts and intents of man's heart were only evil continually." The next new technology achievement was the building of Noah's Ark. It rests in modern Turkey. The United States has a modern military base there, even now.

Time Period Two: Conscience

After Noah and his family increased the population of Earth so greatly, it came to be called community. This means property is owned by all the people at once: one language, one government, one race, one money (one bank), one religion. Religion holds it all together, like family. So, the population decided to build a high tower to Heaven, for they had building technology, the community owned all the material, and they could do the job together.

They could find out if there was a God up there, and they could say they had reached Heaven all by themselves. God did not approve of their arrogant attitude and evil lifestyles, so as only God could, He confounded their language. Then no one could understand his neighbor, and they had to stop the building. Now they were different races. They called it Babylon (confusion). That meant they had to work for themselves without subsistence from anyone else. Now they had to make a new technology; they called it war. At first they fought one race against another race.

Then they developed more technology by joining two or more races together against another race (nation). Now we can see the very first attempt to establish ONE-MAN RULE over the whole inhabited Earth. The KING ENSLAVED ALL THE PEOPLE FOR HIS GAIN. Ancient records tell us there has always been *someone wanting to be that king.* It came to pass in the days of Amraphel, king of Shinar (modern Iraq); Arioch, king of Ellasar; Chedorlaomer, king of Elam (Iran); and *TIDAL,* king of nations (collective/community). These made WAR with Bera, king of Sodom, and with Shinab, king of Admah, the king of Zeboiim, and the king of Bela, who was Zoar (Genesis 14:1). This is the first recorded WAR of history. It was made possible by the formation of a collective system that we might call *The OLD World Order.*

This system, with slight variations, has been within man's governance for ages. Races developed national sovereign rule as the population expanded into Europe, Asia, and Africa. In time, one nation would become prominent and begin to *collect* (make a collective of) smaller, weaker nations. Egypt was able to gain this power through an international famine. Egypt had survived it by collecting and storing food, preparing for the time when the famine became deadly. The

Nation of Israel moved into Egypt and was captive for 430 years. The people called Israel grew from 70 to a vast number; we do not know how many. They were delivered in a most miraculous way from Egypt by Moses into their Promised Land. There they became, and are, a nation like no other on Earth. That was about 4,000 years ago.

A later recorded attempt to rule the world was in ancient Assyria (now Syria); it was north and west of what is now called Asia Minor. Their language was Anatolian: Adjacent to Babylon (now Iraq). Syria's expansion was through Israel all the way to Egypt. (It is of great interest that former President Obama stated over national television, "I am of good Anatolian Stock.") This information tells us that we are in the last stages of *completion* of the NEW WORLD ORDER. Ancient Babylon became *Mystery Babylon, the Great Global System.* Now the world is waiting for that ruler.

Ancient Babylon destroyed ISRAEL'S Temple (600 B.C.), taking the immense riches of gold and silver and the wealthy and royal population into captivity. That king became the richest one of all nations on Earth.

Babylon: The king made a statue of gold, silver, bronze, and iron, with a gold head representing himself. He made his statue 90 feet tall. It was symbolic of the nations that followed him in time to become *like* the NEW WORLD ORDER, which must be GLOBAL.

From that beginning they became Media Persia (Iran), GREECE (led by Alexander the Great), and then ROME, which destroyed Israel's Temple in 70 A.D. and scattered the remaining Jewish people all over the world. Their land was barren and then occupied by others for 1,800-plus years. In these past centuries, numerous rulers have sought to bring in a completed global government in becoming head of Planet Earth.

Time Period 3: Israel's Friend

In 1776, a new nation was founded on the continent of North America called THE UNITED STATES OF AMERICA. This changed the history of the entire world, and the *TECHNOLOGY OF THE WORLD. The CONSTITUTION of the USA SPECIFICALLY STATES two things that make it different from all other countries. They are IN GOD WE TRUST and THE PEOPLE'S RIGHT TO OWN AND BEAR ARMS SHALL NOT BE INFRINGED.* The ultimate power to maintain the Constitution belongs to the people. The foremost power of the nation is its money. The U.S. is the richest nation on Earth, AND THE REST OF THE WORLD WANTS THOSE RICHES. Think back in history to the time when the country was founded. The technology was very ancient. There were sailing ships, very crude firearms, and horses. Then came the continental (Civil) war, with its steam engines and railroads. Then at the turn of the century, at the time of World War I, there were airplanes!

Then there was mechanical technology. Mathematical understanding went way up. Then near the end of the war, Woodrow Wilson became president of the U.S. He began to organize what he called the *LEAGUE OF NATIONS*. All nations had to sign into the League. But there was a problem; they would lose their sovereignty. That system faild.

Phase 1 of the war against liberty was thus put into operation. A new generation had to appear well educated in the Marxist socialist ways of GLOBAL SYSTEM RULE. During World War II, technology began to multiply, with electronics, sonar, and jet engines. As crude as they were, *COMPUTERS* also came along, as did the *ATOMIC BOMB*. The war ended in 1945. The electronic transistor was developed by a U.S. scientist after World War II. President Franklin Roosevelt, Winston Churchill, and Joseph Stalin organized the *UNITED NATIONS*. Their published propaganda was "Peace in the world," but their real goal was and *IS GLOBAL RULE. It was charted to be a collective monopoly. The first thing the organization did was appoint the richest seven nations' heads of government, called the G7,* as the ruling body. Other nations were added with time. It should be of interest that JAPAN surrendered to the UNITED NATIONS on the deck of the Battleship *U.S.S. MISSOURI* at the end of World War II.

The first signer of the U.N. Charter was China. President Harry Truman, for the U.S., signed the document that made ISRAEL A NEW NATION May 15, 1948. Since that day, many nations have sought to destroy Israel by war. The nations fought several wars and lost each and every one. The nation of Israel has developed the latest military technology. They have one of the strongest militaries (and likely the atomic bomb) on Earth. In the U.S., the new world order team is fighting a war of subversion by planting their operatives in government systems.

They were to destroy the U.S. Constitution, filling the federal government with members who hold liberal political views. The program was so successful they could continue with Phase 2 of the program, which was started by a past president when he went to China and gave them our manufacturing companies so the U.S. had to buy their products at extremely high prices. Then the U.S. government went on wild, outrageous spending sprees, inflating the dollar to almost worthless levels. Now Phase 3: Take away the people's civil liberties with unconstitutional laws, which the Supreme Court ignores. The U.S. now has more than 150 military bases overseas to protect those nations free of charge to them at the expense of U.S. taxpayer dollars, and no one will tell us the true sum of our national debt. But we know that it exceeds $120 trillion.

Phase 4: Christians Must Be Eliminated

The new world order has several ways to eliminate Christians. The first step is to start successive foreign wars at great expense of the people's money, and at the same time, *reduce in great numbers the population of Earth. Immigrants must be forced to illegally migrate to the wealthy countries. Just one part of the plan to destroy the liberty of the host nation is by gradually replacing the existing government with socialists, thereby redistributing the wealth and destroying the Constitution's liberty for the nation.* In ancient times, the Assyrian's (the future Antichrist's) program of expansion was invasion of Israel on his way to take over all nations. His plan was repopulation of the Earth at the same time. President Trump opposes the U.N. plan to *replace* the U.S. population, yet the Catholic Charities, Lutheran Social Services, and the resettlement agencies go to leaders to notify them of their intent to send refugees. They tell how they will open businesses and boost the local economy, which is far from reality. For instance, Minnesota approved an additional $600,000 to treat infectious diseases among refugees. And for the Somali refugees the amount was $1.5 million — the cost of children's education. This system has the official policy of the Communist Party. It claims it is saving the Earth. They have signed this agreement with most nations. President Trump has signed off. The following is a copy of the United States Department of State PUBLICATION #7277 SERIES 5, September 1961:

FREEDOM FROM WAR: UNITED STATES PROGRAM FOR GENERAL AND COMPLETE DISARMAMENT IN A PEACEFUL WORLD Stage 1. All States will have adhered to a treaty effectively prohibiting the testing of nuclear weapons and on … Stage 2 …. Civilian arms will be banned except for police and internal peacekeeping.

The document has six pages of regulations that effectively hand all power to the commander of United Nation Forces. It is easy to see why the socialists are pushing for removing civilian arms. History shows us how their system murders the innocent. By country, here are some of the deaths attributed to each: Ottoman Turkey, 1915, 1 million to 1.5 million deaths; Soviet Union, 1925-45, 20 million deaths; Nazis

(German National Socialists), 1933-45, 20 million deaths; Nationalist China, 1927, 10 million deaths; Communist China, 1949-76, 40 million deaths (U.S. Library of Congress); Cambodia, 1975-79, 2 million deaths.

The list goes on. The message is clear: Giving up civilian weapons has deathly consequences. The next problem they had to solve was that the premier of post-war Russia made this statement on international television: "We cannot have a New World Order without *religion*." One of the top communists in the world made this statement! Now there would be a single religion that the world could come to accept. And it now has been devised and agreed upon by the largest groups, though it took a long time for the elements to agree: In December 2006, Mahmoud Ahmadinejad, president of Iran, made this statement to the world: He expects both Jesus and the Shiite messianic figure, Imam Mahdi, to return to Earth and wipe away oppression. This seems impossible at first glance, but we have another document quoting evangelical leaders' pledge for *COMMON CAUSE*. Yale Divinity School, endorsed by other liberal Christian leaders, apologized for the sins of Christians in the Crusades, and even seemed to acknowledge the Muslim god as the God of the Bible. This obvious sellout seems impossible, but now we have another voice, which was shown on the internet: the Pope's travel to the Islamic center for a conference with the leader of Islam. The Pope was cordially received, but no conversation was allowed to be heard. This we know: There are more than a billion Catholics on Earth and more than a billion Muslims. Since they have accord, they will have a single doctrine and articles of faith. The Pope revealed them to the world over the internet. Briefly stated, it says to the U.S. Congress (paraphrased) that everyone is equal and therefore there is no difference; there is no hell, and therefore everyone must go to Heaven. Since Jesus died for the world, all the world is forgiven. We each live in a way that seems right to us. It matters not how or who we worship since we are one world.

This is an incredible description of the Hebrew-written Holy Bible where it says, "Now the Spirit expressly says that in latter times some shall depart from the faith, giving heed to deceiving spirits and doctrines of devils" (1 Timothy 4:1). This is a perfect description of right now, for the religious world we live in is now waiting for the completed system. We can now show the details of the beginning, present, and future, with the *technology we now have, to the END of the* New World Order, and chronology, as it fits the history of the HEBREW NATION ISRAEL. Remember the Ancient Assyrian's plan is repeated in the very near future by the coming appearance of the modern Antichrist. According to the written records of the Hebrew prophet Habakkuk, chapter 2, "He cannot be satisfied but gathers to him (as head of the U.N.) ALL nations and ALL people." This was written 626 B.C. and confirmed by an Apostle's records written in 33-98 A.D. Paul the Apostle states, "That wicked man of sin will be revealed; he opposes God and exalts himself above all that is worshiped so that he sits in Israel's Temple; *showing HIMSELF to be a god that must be worshiped.*" This requires two things that must happen in the very near future: ONE, the Hebrew prophet Daniel describes the NEW WORLD ORDER as we know it today as the global commercial trade of TEN nations (and their Satellite groups), on which a former U.S. President insisted, "We must continue to use Global Trade." TWO, this man of sin (THE ANTICHRIST) must come from among these ten nations.

The establishment is shown in the Bible record as a man sitting upon a scarlet-colored "beast," full of names of blasphemy and having seven heads and ten horns. This sign pictures a statue in front of the headquarters of the European Union in Brussels, Belgium, which is part of the United Nations, which has the G7 heads and ten kings (and kingdoms). The beast itself is the Assyrian (Antichrist). The head of the picture depicts the global MYSTERY BABYLON THE GREAT, THE MOTHER OF HARLOTS AND ABOMINATIONS OF THE EARTH. This entire system is responsible for the blood of all who are slain on the Earth, through countless wars and other criminal acts. There are many ways of warfare. The Hebrew Apostle Matthew wrote these words of Jesus about 33 A.D.: "Nation will rise against nation and kingdom against kingdom: and there will be famines, and plagues and earthquakes in various places, all these are the *beginning of sorrows*" (Matthew 24:8). We see this plague as the CORONAVIRUS. Now (in 2020 A.D.) upon every nation on Earth, coronavirus is a vicious killer of hundreds of thousands now and is still going. The Hebrew Prophet Isaiah in 600 B.C. stated, "The day of the Lord of hosts shall be upon everyone that is proud and lofty and everything lifted up, and it shall be brought low … upon all the ships of Tarshish (now Tartus in Syria), pleasant (Pleasure) ships" (Isaiah 2:8). In 2020 we saw the pleasure ships looking for a place to dock with their numerous CORONAVIRUS-infected passengers. The world was warned of it 2,600 years ago. The Merchants of Tarshish are in existence now and in the actual Day of the Lord, which does not begin until the Nation of Israel signs a *treaty of death* with the Antichrist/Assyrian. As far as we know now, that has not happened, but we do know the Lord will cancel their covenant of death. Isaiah tells us all about it in 28:15:

"Because you have said, We have made a covenant with death, and with Hell we are in agreement; when the overflowing scourge shall pass through, it shall not come to us: for we have made lies our refuge, and under falsehood we have hid ourselves." But God said your covenant with Death shall be annulled … but the sorrows of the beginning will continue for seven years. Those seven years will be great punishments upon the world and Israel. In the news May 14, 2020, the prime minister of Israel said he would annex the West Bank to Israeli sovereignty within eighteen months. Then another party in Israel takes rule until the next election. The sorrows and troubles of Israel will increase through the future tribulation of seven years. We must be aware of God's *time clock, Israel: We can see in His plan and purpose of two things* we find in the record of God and His Hebrew prophets. Witness: You are my witnesses. I and the ***children whom the Lord has given me are for signs and wonders in Israel from the Lord of Hosts.*** **You are my witnesses, says the Lord, and my servant whom I have chosen: that you may know and believe me, and understand that I am he: before me there was no God formed, neither shall there be after me. I even I am the Lord; and beside me there is no savior** (Isaiah 43:10-11).

God's Temple will be built in Mount Zion. This is the city of David. Ruins of that site can be seen now; they are 600 feet from the mountain of the dome of the rock. The dome was never built on the temple's true site. The first temple, built by King Solomon, was in the city of David, which is Mount Zion. The latest discovery has been found in that city: two column chapiters with King David's signature carved on them. This means the site of the New Temple is in Israeli control, therefore the Muslim dome site would not be disturbed. The Temple of Israel will be built. The prime minister has made the statement, "I will build the temple." Before that can happen, they must sign the covenant of death. They will sign it.

Plans for construction of the temple are given by the Prophet Ezekiel. Certain conditions must be in place before the signing of the covenant: First, Israel must accept loss of sovereignty for peace, even receiving the Assyrian (Antichrist, Beast) as their Messiah (Madai). Second, his identity must be revealed to the world. Then he will take ruling power over nations of Earth. Third, the church of the Lord Jesus Christ must be prepared and ready to meet Him in the air when He appears at His return. At the same time, certain 144,000 of the tribes of Israel will be instantly saved and prepared to preach the Gospel of the Kingdom on Earth to a world of hate and death. This event is the beginning of the worst seven years of humankind's history: the TRIBULATION. At the height of human technology achievements, he begins to receive the maximum destruction of those days, for *then* shall be great tribulation, such as was not since the beginning of the world to this time, no, nor ever shall be. And unless those days would be shortened, no flesh would survive (Matthew 24:22). They will receive the Antichrist's mark (computer chip ID) under the skin, in the hand or forehead, where it is *Required to buy and sell.* The last three-and-one-half years, called "the Great tribulation," will bring destruction, pollution, and climate change so vast, the Green Party movement never dreamed it could be possible. The details are described in the eternal record in great detail. We go forward now to the beginning of the TRIBUALTION, when Israel's tribes, saved and sealed by God, must endure and preach the gospel of the Kingdom: "And after these things I saw four *angels* standing on the four corners of the Earth, holding the four winds of the Earth, that the wind on the Earth, nor on the sea, nor on any tree" (Revelation 7:1+).

And I saw another *angel* ascending from the east, having the seal of the living God: and he cried with a loud voice to the four *angels*, to whom it was given to hurt the Earth and the sea, saying hurt not the Earth, neither the sea, nor the trees, till we have sealed the servants of our God in their foreheads.

And I heard the number of them which were sealed: and there were sealed an hundred and forty and four thousand of all the tribes of the children of Israel. Of the tribe of Judah were sealed twelve thousand. Of the tribe of Reuben were sealed twelve thousand. Of the tribe of Gad were sealed twelve thousand. Of the tribe of Aser were sealed twelve thousand. Of the tribe of Nepthalim were sealed twelve thousand. Of the tribe of Manasses. Of the tribe of Simeon were sealed twelve thousand. Of the tribe of Levi were sealed twelve thousand. Of the tribe of Issachar were sealed twelve thousand. Of the tribe of Zabulon. Of the tribe of Joseph were sealed twelve thousand. Of the tribe of Benjamin were sealed twelve thousand. … After this I beheld a great multitude which no man could number, of all nations, kindreds and peoples, and tongues, stood before the throne, and before the Lamb, clothed with white robes, and palms in their hands. And cried with a loud voice, saying, Salvation is of our God who sits upon the throne, and unto the Lamb …. This sealing is in the future. This 144,000 is the first fruits (first part of Israel). The rest of Israel. Two groups called ALL ISRAEL. We now return to our day ….

The wealth of all the Earth must be collected, combined, and deposited in the World's Bank. Its money can only be withdrawn by use of the chip; however, there is wealth on Earth that is not deposited in that bank, such as oil, natural gas, chemicals, and even clean water. We can now look at the plan of the Assyrian (Antichrist) for robbery of the nations, which begins, according to the Hebrew Prophet Isaiah. Chapter 10:5-25 tells us, "O Assyrian the rod of my anger. He does not mean so, nor does his heart think so; but it is in his heart to destroy and cut off nations not a few when the Lord has performed his whole work on Mount Zion and Jerusalem. I will punish the fruit of the arrogant heart of the king of Assyria and the glory of his high looks, for he says: 'By the strength of my hand have I done it, and by my wisdom, for I am prudent; also ***I have removed the boundaries of all of the people, and robbed their treasuries; so I have put down the inhabitants like a valiant man. My hand has found like a nest the riches of the people, and as one that gathers eggs that are left, I have gathered all the Earth's; and there was no one who moved his wing, nor opened his mouth with even a peep.'***" We certainly will not forget the words of a former President of the U.S.A. who made these words his policy: ***He will redistribute the wealth,*** as he campaigned for the office: *These words are being carried out exactly as spoken 2,500 years ago.* The globalists have always been against Israel. They have one policy that never changes: the further we get into the Tribulation, the more they hate Israel and the people of the U.S.A. The wealth of the world is a great concern of a group called the TEN KINGS. Remembering the Merchants of Tartus who use the Ships of Tartus, Russian ships are now based in the city of Tartus, Syria. We can now identify where they are and what they do. They are revealed in the Book of Revelation Chapter 18 (within the tribulation). They are used after the *end of the tribulation to transport remaining Jewish people to Israel (Isaiah 60:9).*

And another *angel* came down from Heaven, having great power; and the Earth was illuminated with his glory. And he cried mightily with a loud voice, saying, "Babylon the great is fallen, and has become a dwelling place of demons, a prison for every foul spirit, and a cage for every unclean and hated bird. For all nations have drank of the wine of the wrath of her fornication (becoming rich), and the *kings of the Earth have committed fornication; this means everything bad, for a nation; it means treason with her, and the merchants have become rich through the abundance of her luxury."* I heard another voice saying, "Come out of her, **my people, lest you share in her sins."** We have another picture of these treasonous "deals" made by the rulers of the New World Order. Seen in Ezekiel 38, "Now the word of the Lord came to me saying, 'Son of man, set your face against Gog, of the land of Magog, the prince of Rosh, Meshech, and Tubal, then prophesy against him: and say, "Thus says the Lord God: 'Behold, I am against you, O Gog the prince of Rosh, Meshech, and Trubal. I will turn you around, put hooks into your jaws, and lead you out, with all splendid clothing, a great company with bucklers and shields, all of them handling swords. Persia, (Iran) Ethiopia, and Libya are with them, all of them with shield and helmet; Gomer with all its troops … many people are with you. Prepare yourself and be ready, you and all your companies that are gathered about you, and be a guard for them.'

""After many days you will be visited. In the latter years you will come into the land of those brought back from the sword and gathered from many people on the mountains of Israel, which had long been desolate; they were brought back out of the nations, and now all of them dwell safely. You will ascend, coming like a storm, covering the land like a cloud, you and your troops and many peoples with you. … You will say, 'I will go up against the land with unwalled villages; I will go to a peaceful people, who dwell safely, all of them dwelling without walls, and having neither bars nor gates … to people **gathered from the nations, who have acquired livestock and goods who dwell in the midst of the land.**"" **Sheba, Dedan, the Merchants of** Tarshish, which equals Tartus (in Syria) (Note: In September of 2020, Israel demanded that Hamas be removed from Syria) **and all their YOUNG LIONS will say to you, have you come to take plunder? Have you gathered your army to take booty, to carry away silver and**

gold, to take away livestock and goods, to take great plunder? The young Lions are the ten kings of the global commercial trade system we now live in. They betray their own countries for personal gain. The commercial kings/kingdoms are as follows: 1. USA/CANADA/MEXICO 2. WESTERN EUROPE 3. JAPAN/KOREA 4. AUSTRALIA 5. EASTERN EUROPE 6. SOUTH/AMERICA 7. ISLAMIC NATIONS 8. AFRICA/ETHIOPIA 9. INDIA 10. CHINA.

Domestic commercial systems do not invade Israel yet for themselves, but individual ***NATIONS do. God himself calls them to this battle in Ezekiel 38:13-23 He will bring them against Israel; HE destroys them. Verse 18 states that when Gog (Russia) shall come against the land of Israel, says the Lord God, my fury shall come up in my face, for in my jealousy and in the fire of my wrath have I spoken, in that day there shall be a great shaking in the land of Israel … all the men on Earth shall shake at my presence and the mountains shall be thrown down, and the steep places will fall, and every wall shall fall to the ground."***

The wrath of God continues, "So I will make my holy name known in the midst of my people Israel; and I will not let them pollute my holy name any more: and the heathen shall know that I am the Lord, the Holy

One in Israel." **When God's** wrath is magnified to great extent by the Prophet Isaiah in 13:13, when God takes Earth **out of orbit**, climate change and Earth pollution will increase beyond description. This part of the WAR against Israel begins in the middle of the seven years of the tribulation: but God sends a series of wars of judgment on the whole Earth. Apostle John tells us what happens:

> And there appeared a great wonder in heaven; a woman (ISRAEL), clothed with the sun, and the moon under her feet and upon her head a crown of twelve stars (the twelve tribes). … And there appeared another wonder in heaven; and behold a great red dragon having seven heads and ten horns (Satan and the New World Order), and seven crowns (the G7) upon his heads …. (Revelation 12:1+).

She brought forth a man child (Christ) who was to rule ALL nations with a rod of iron: and her child was caught up unto God, and to his throne. … And the serpent (Satan) cast out of his mouth water as a flood (the invasion by Gog) after the woman, that he might cause her to be carried away of the flood. BUT Israel

BURIED the flood of HUMAN FLESH that dares to fight against the living God.

The nation of Israel and all nations endures SEVEN WARS in the last three-and-one-half years of the Great Tribulation. The WARS are global; none will escape them. The first one is begun in Israel: "And the dragon was enraged with the woman and he went to make WAR with the rest of her offspring, who keep the commandments of God and have the testimony of Jesus Christ." This WAR of the Antichrist is against all the Christians of the tribulation: And he and all men and women will have faced the judgment of God as he pours punishment on those who hate God and have rejected His written Word. We see the formation of the system that is to be judged in the tribulation: As it was in ancient times, it began with Babylon, then Media Persia, Greece, Rome. In our time frame 6,000 years later, old and NEW NAMES: IRAQ, IRAN, GREECE, ITALY. The first war fought while Israel is protected by God in the Wilderness. And there was a WAR in heaven: Michael and his *angels* fought against the dragon (Satan); and the dragon fought and *his* angels, and prevailed not, neither was their place found in heaven. And the great dragon was cast out, that old serpent, called the Devil, and Satan, which *deceives the whole world:* He was cast out into the Earth, and his angels were cast out with him (Revelation 12:7+).

And I heard a loud voice saying in Heaven: Now is come salvation, and strength, and the kingdom of our God, and the power of his Christ; for the accuser of our brethren is cast down, who accused them before our God day and night. And they overcame him by the blood of the Lamb, and by the word of their testimony; and they loved not their lives unto death. Therefore rejoice thou heavens, and you that dwell in them.

Woe, to the inhabiters of Earth and the sea! For the Devil is come down to you, having great wrath, because he knows that he has but a short time. This is one of three woes that happens in the tribulation. The dragon was angry with the woman, and went to make WAR with the remnant of her seed, which have the commandments of God, and have the testimony of Jesus Christ. ... The woes of the devil are now on the people (Revelation 12:12).

This Satanic *system is put into place.* John the Apostle and recorder writes the following: And I stood upon the sand of the sea (Mediterranean), and saw a beast rise up out of the sea, having *Seven Heads and Ten Horns (the New World Order)! "I considered the horns* *(kings), and behold there came up among them another little horn, before whom there were three of the **first were plucked up by the roots,** and, behold in this horn were eyes like the eyes of a man, and a mouth speaking great things* (Daniel 7:8). The United Nations was created in 1942 by Winston Churchill, Franklin Roosevelt, and Joseph Stalin. At the end of World War II, the G7 heads (of nations) were added to rebuild the war damage. The nations are U.S.A., BRITAIN, CANADA, FRANCE, GERMANY, JAPAN, and ITALY. Every U.S.A. president (head) has been one of the G7 members. Note: There came up among them two U.S. Presidents that have been SHOT, JOHN F KENNEDY and RONALD REAGAN. Reagan survived and finished his term and retired. We can expect another G7 head to be "plucked up" between now and the end of the tribulation.

Peace on Earth is the desire of the United Nations (according to their policy). How strange it is, then, that there has been war after war since World War II, where in most cases U.N. troops were sent in to bring peace. WHY? The New World Order must be *completed first.* It must have one man to rule the world of more than 7 billion people. We can see the coming of that man in the ancient records: "For the *mystery* of lawlessness already works; only (there is) one who restrains now; until he be taken out of the way; and then that lawless one shall be *revealed* whom the Lord shall consume with the breath of his mouth, and shall destroy by the brightness of his coming; *even him*, whose coming is after the **working of Satan** with all power and signs and lying wonders, and with all deceivableness of unrighteousness in those that perish because they received not the love of the truth that they could be saved" (2 Thessalonians 2:7-13).

Note that the wisest man that ever lived spoke these words: "You are of your father the Devil … for he is a liar, and the father of it (the Liar). This mystery ruler must come from the ten kings, with a mouth speaking great things." Without question many lies are fed to the people daily. The Antichrist must reveal himself, and that is easy because of his great popularity among the people; this is the way he appears using technology:

> When the Lamb opened one of the seals, I heard as it were the noise of thunder, one of the four living creatures saying, come and see. And I saw and: behold a white horse: and he that sat up him had a bow; and a crown was *given him*: and he went forth conquering and to conquer. (Revelation 6)

He presents himself to be the promised messiah, and he has awesome military power. "*Who can make WAR with him?*" This is confirmed by the prophet Daniel: "And the king shall do according to his will; and he shall exalt himself and magnify *himself* above every god, and shall speak marvelous things against the God of gods, and shall prosper; he shall not regard the God of his fathers, nor the desire of women, nor regard any god: for he will magnify himself above all. Will he do in the most strongholds with a heathen god, whom he will *acknowledge and increase* with glory: and he will cause them to rule over many, and will divide the land for gain (profit)." And he causes all, both small and great, rich and poor, free and bond, to receive a mark in their right hand, or in their foreheads: And that no man might buy or sell except he that had the mark, or the name of the beast, or the number of his name. Note the three woes: Revelation 8 to 9:12, 11:14, and 12:12.

WARS OF ANGELS Rev 8:2+: And the seven angels which had the seven trumpets prepared themselves to sound. The *first angel* sounded and there followed hail and fire mingled with blood, and they were cast upon the Earth: and the third part of trees were burnt up. And all green grass was upon the Earth: and the third part of trees was burnt up, and all green grass was burnt up.

And the *second angel* sounded and as it were a great mountain burning with fire was cast into the sea: and the third part of the sea became blood; And the creatures which were in the sea and had life died; and a third part of the ships were destroyed.

The *third angel* sounded and there fell a great star from heaven burning as it were a lamp, and it fell upon the third part of the rivers. And upon the fountains of waters; and the name of the star is called wormwood: the third part of the waters became wormwood; and many men died of the waters, because they were bitter.

And the *fourth angel* sounded. And the third part of the sun was smitten, and the third part of the moon, and a third part of the stars; so the third part of them was darkened, and the day shown not for a third part of it, and the night likewise. And I beheld, and heard an *angel* flying through the midst of heaven, saying with a loud voice, "Woe, woe, woe, to the inhabiters of the Earth by reason of the other voices of the trumpet of the three angels which are yet to sound!"

And the *fifth angel* sounded. Revelation 9:1+ states the following: I saw a star fall from heaven to the Earth:

and to him was given the key of the bottomless pit. And he opened the bottomless pit; and there arose out of the pit, as the smoke of a great furnace; and the sun and the air were darkened by reason of the smoke of the pit. And there came out of the smoke locusts upon the Earth: and to them was given power as the scorpions of the Earth have power. And to them it was commanded them that they should not hurt the grass of the Earth neither any green thing, neither any tree; but only those men which have not the seal of God in their foreheads. And to them it was given that they not kill them, but that they should be tormented five months and their torment was as a scorpion, when he strikes a man. And in those days shall men seek death, and they shall not find it; and shall desire to die.

And death shall flee from them. And the shapes of the locusts were like unto horses prepared unto battle; and on their heads crowns like gold and their faces were as the faces of men. And they had hair as the hair of women, and their teeth were as the teeth of lions. And they had breast plates of iron; and the sound of their wings as the sound of chariots of many horses running to battle. And they had tails like scorpions, and there were stings in their tails: and their power was to hurt men five months. And they had king over them which is the angel of the bottomless pit, whose name in the Hebrew tongue is Abaddon, but in the Greek tongue his name is Apollyon. One woe is past (WARS OF ANGELS, *Revelation 9:15+*).

There are many more of these plagues from the bottomless pit … the prison house of demons, devils, of whom Satan is king. But **the Lord Jesus Christ has the key to it!** There are many more pictures of the punishment of God upon men who hate Him. He describes this society of man even now …. And the rest of the men which were not killed by these plagues, yet repented not of the *works of their hands, that they should not worship devils, and idols of gold and silver, and brass, and of wood: which can neither can see, nor hear, nor walk: Neither did they repent of their murders nor their sorceries (Greek: Pharmakeia, drugs), nor of their fornication nor of their thefts* (Revelation 9:15-21).

And there was a WAR in heaven. Michael and his *angels* fought against the dragon; (Satan) fought and his angels; and prevailed not; neither was their place found any more in heaven. And the great dragon was cast out into the Earth, and his angels were cast out with him and the serpent cast out of his mouth water as a flood … and the Earth helped the woman and the Earth upon her mouth and swallowed up the flood;

and the dragon was angry with the woman and went to make WAR with the remnant of her seed, which keep the commandments of God, and have the testimony of Jesus Christ (Revelation 12:7).

Daniel the prophet writes: I saw in the night visions, and beheld a fourth beast, dreadful and terrible, exceedingly strong. It had huge iron teeth; it was devouring, breaking in pieces and stamped the residue with the feet of it: and it was diverse from all the beasts that were before it; and it *had ten horns*. I considered the horns and behold there came up *among them another little horn, before whom three of the of the first horns were plucked up by the roots: and, behold, in this horn were eyes like eyes of a man, and a mouth speaking great things.*

Daniel saw this 2,500 years ago. There are details intentionally left out. That vision can only be understood at a later time. (I explain it later in the proper time frame.) And saw a BEAST rise up out of the sea (the Mediterranean) having [seven heads and ten horns,] and upon his horns ten crowns, and upon his heads the name of blasphemy … and the dragon gave him his power, and his throne, and great authority. And I saw one of his heads as it were wounded to death; and his deadly wound was healed: and all the world wondered after the beast. And they worshiped the dragon which gave power unto the beast, saying (in Rev 13:1+) …

Who is like unto the beast; who is able to make WAR with him? And there was given unto him a mouth speaking great things and blasphemies; and power was given unto him to continue forty-two months …. And it was given unto him to make WAR with the saints (of God), and overcome them: and power was given him over all kindreds, and tongues, and nations, and all that that dwell on the Earth shall worship him, whose names are not written in the book of life of the lamb slain from the foundation of the world. "If anyone have an ear, let him hear." Here is wisdom; let him who has understanding calculate the number of the beast, for it is the number of a man: His number is 666. The Apple computer handbook has an instruction page that tells us how to open the program: F666 hexadecimal. To begin from the monitor, enter the command 666. This access has to be changed from hexadecimal to the binomial Base 2 for our use. The calculation follows (add remainders):

$$666/2 = 333 \times 2 = 666 \text{ Subtract From } 666 = 0$$
$$333/2 = 166 \times 2 = 332 \dots \dots 333 = 1$$

$$166/2 = 83\times2 = 166 \ldots \ldots 166 = 0$$
$$83/2 = 41\times2 = 82 \ldots \ldots 83 = 1$$
$$41/2 = 20\times2 = 40 \ldots \ldots 40 = 1$$
$$20/2 = 10\times2 = 20 \ldots \ldots 20 = 0$$
$$10/2 = 5\times2 = 10 \ldots \ldots 10 = 0$$
$$5/2 = 2\times2 = 4 \ldots \ldots 5 = 1$$
$$2/2 = 2\times1 = 2 \ldots \ldots 2 = 0$$
$$\tfrac{1}{2} = 1\times0 = 1 \ 0 \ 1 = 1$$

The number 666 = 10110011010 — the computer number of the Man-Beast. Revelation 13:18 adds, *And ALL his worshippers.*

Consider the example of Three Square Market, which has microchipped its employees: Three Square Market became the first U.S. company to provide microchip technology to their employees on August 1, 2017. These employees have been implanted with a chip the size of a grain of rice, and the chip allows them to make purchases in their break room market, to open doors, to log in to computers, to use the copy machine, etc. This system is ***now in use on a VOLUNTARY basis in many foreign countries.*** The 666 number implant will be MANDATORY to buy and sell in the Great Tribulation.

And I beheld another beast coming up out of the Earth; and he had two horns like a lamb and he spoke as a dragon. And he exercises all the power of the first beast (Antichrist) before him, and causes the Earth and those who dwell therein to worship the first beast, whose deadly wound was healed. And he does great wonders, so that he makes fire come down from heaven on the Earth in the sight of men and deceives those that dwell on the Earth by the means of those miracles which he had power to do, saying that they should make an image to the beast which had a wound by a sword and did live. Now we see the New World Religion at work in the New World Order (Revelation 13:11). And I looked, and lo, a Lamb stood on the Mount Zion (Revelation 14:1) and with him an hundred and forty and four thousand, having his Father's name written in their foreheads (from Revelation 7:4, where they were sealed by God.)

And I heard a voice from heaven, as the voice of many waters, and as a voice of a great thunder: and I heard the voice harpers harping with their harps: and they sung as it were a new song before the throne, and before the four living creatures, and the elders: and no man could learn that song but the hundred and forty and four thousand, which were redeemed from the Earth. These are they which are not defiled with women; for they are virgins. These are they which follow the Lamb wherever he goes. These were redeemed from among men, being the first fruits (Romans 11:16) unto God and the Lamb. And in their mouth was found no guile: for they are without fault before the throne of God.

Revelation 14:8 continues: And there followed another *angel* saying, Babylon is fallen, that great city. Because she made all nations drink of the wine of the wrath of her fornication. And the third *angel* followed them, saying with a loud voice, if any man worship the beast and his image, and receive his mark in his forehead, or in his hand, the same shall drink of the wrath of God, which is poured out without mixture into the cup of his indignation; and he shall be tormented with fire and brimstone in the presence of the holy *angels,* and in the presence of the Lamb. And the smoke of their torment ascends up forever and ever; and they have no rest day nor night, who worship the beast and his image. And whoever receives the mark of his name … (Revelation 14:11). Here is the patience of the saints: here are they that keep the commandments of God, and the faith of Jesus. And I heard a voice from heaven saying unto me, "Write, blessed are the dead which die in the Lord from henceforth: Yes, says the Spirit, that they may rest from their labors; and their works do follow them."

And I looked, and behold and a white cloud, and upon the cloud one sat like unto the son of man, having on his head a golden crown, and in his hand a sharp sickle. And another *angel* came out of the temple, crying with a loud voice to him that sat on the cloud, "Thrust in thy sickle, and reap: for the time is come for thee to reap; for the harvest of the earth is ripe. And he that sat on the cloud thrust in his sickle on the earth; and the earth was reaped." As the author, I must interrupt, to show there is a **time of seven years between the** first sickle and the second: The white cloud is representing the *harvest* of the saved (grapes) of the tribulation and occurs at the end of the seven years, where they go into the 1,000 years of peace, the Kingdom of David. Luke 1:30-32 offers a message from the *Angel: "And the Angel said to her; Fear not, Mary: for you have found favor with God. And, behold, thou shall conceive in thy womb, and shall bring forth a son and, and shall call his name* **JESUS.** And he shall be great, and shall be called the son of the highest: and the Lord God shall give unto him the throne of his father David. And he shall reign over the house of Jacob forever; and of his kingdom there shall be no end." The true church of Jesus is taken up to meet him in the cloud at the time BEFORE the tribulation (1 Thessalonians 4:13-17).

Now the second sickle: Revelation 14:18 states the following: "And another *angel* came out of the temple which is in heaven, he also having a sharp sickle. And another *angel came out from the altar*, which had power over fire; and cried with a loud cry to him that has the sharp sickle, saying, Thrust in thy sharp sickle, and **gathe**r the clusters of the vine of the Earth; for her grapes are fully ripe. And the *angel* thrust his sickle into the Earth, and gathered the vine of the Earth, and cast it into the great winepress of the wrath of God. And the winepress was trodden (without, apart from) the city, and blood came out of the winepress even to the horse's bridles, by the space of a thousand six hundred furlongs."

As written in the Scripture, And I saw another sign in heaven, great and marvelous, *seven angels,* having the seven last plagues, for in them is filled up the wrath of God. "And I saw as it were a sea of glass mingled with fire, and those who had gotten the VICTORY over the beast and over his image, and over his mark, and over the number of his name, stand on the sea of glass, having the harps of God. And they sing the song of Moses the servant of God, and the Song of the Lamb, saying, Great and marvelous are your works, Lord God Almighty; just and true are thy ways, thou King of Saints" (Revelation 15:1-2).

Revelation 16:19 states the following: Behold I come as a thief, blessed is he that watches and keeps his garments, lest they walk naked, and they see his shame. And the seventh poured *angel* his vial his vial into the air, and Great Babylon came into remembrance before God, to give to her the cup of the wine of the fierceness of his wrath. And every island fled away, and the mountains were not found. And there fell upon men a great hail out of heaven, every stone about the weight of a talent (about 75 pounds): and men blasphemed God because of the plague of the hail; for the plague was exceeding great. And one of the *angels* which had the seven vials talked with me, saying, come here, I will show you judgment of the great harlot that sits on many waters (people), with whom the kings of the Earth have committed fornication, and the inhabitants of the Earth have been made drunk with the wine of her fornication. So he carried me away into the wilderness, and I saw a woman sit upon a scarlet-colored beast, full of names of blasphemy, having seven heads and ten horns. And the woman was arrayed in purple and scarlet color, and decked with gold and precious stones and pearls, having a golden cup in her hand full of abominations and filthiness of her fornication; and upon her forehead was a name (Revelation 17:5+), written, MYSTERY, BABYLON THE GREAT, THE

MOTHER OF HARLOTS AND ABOMINATIONS OF THE EARTH. And I saw the woman drunken with the blood of the saints, and with the blood of the martyrs of Jesus; and when I saw her I marveled with great amazement. And the *angel* said to me Why did you marvel?

I will tell you the mystery of the of the woman, and of the beast that carries her, which has the seven heads and ten horns: which you saw, are ten kings who have received no kingdom as yet, but they will receive power for seven years, as kings with the Beast. These are of one mind, and they will give their power and authority to the Beast. *These will make WAR* with the Lamb, and the Lamb will overcome them, for He is Lord of lords, and King of kings; and those who are with him are called, chosen, and faithful. Then he said to me, the waters which you saw, where the harlot sits, **are peoples, multitudes, nations, and tongues.** And the ten horns you saw on the beast, these will hate the harlot, make her desolate and naked, and eat her flesh and burn her with fire. For God has put into their hearts to fulfill his will, and to agree and to give their kingdom to the beast, until the words of God are fulfilled. (I would interrupt here to present a reference given us by Daniel the prophet, when he wrote of the

Babylon which had invaded and captured his people Israel: verse 17.) *God Most High rules in the kingdom of men, and gives it to whomever he will, and sets over it the lowest of men (verse 25), till you know that the Most High rules in the kingdom of men, and gives it to whomever he chooses (verse 32).* … And the woman whom you saw is that great city which reigns *over the kings of the Earth.*

After these things (Revelation 18:1), I saw another *angel* coming down, from heaven having great authority, and the earth was illuminated with his glory. And he cried mightily with a loud voice saying, "Babylon the great (global) is fallen, is fallen, and has become a dwelling place of demons, a prison for every foul spirit, and a cage for every unclean and hated bird." The kings of the Earth who committed fornication and *lived luxuriously with her will weep and lament for her, when they see the smoke of her burning.* And I heard another voice from heaven saying, "Come out of her, my people (Israel), lest you share in her sins, and lest you receive of her plagues. Her sins have reached to heaven, and God has remembered her iniquities: *in her was found the blood of prophets and saints, and of all who were slain on the Earth.*"

WARS OF KINGS AND ANGELS (Jeremiah 51:63)

The ancient prophet Jeremiah wrote in a book all the evils that would come upon Babylon. These words are written against Babylon. … When you read all these words; then you shall say, "O Lord, You have spoken against this place to cut it off, so that none will remain in it, neither man nor beast; it shall be desolate forever." Now it shall be when you have finished this book, you shall tie a stone to it and throw into the Euphrates. "Then you shall say, Thus Babylon shall sink and not rise from the catastrophe that I will bring upon her. And they shall be weary."

The *sixth* angel sounded, and I heard a voice from the four horns of the golden altar that is before God, saying to the *sixth angel* which had the trumpet, "Release the *four angels* who are bound at the great river Euphrates." So the four angels, who had been prepared for the hour and a day and month and year were released to kill a third of mankind. Now the number of the army of the horsemen was two hundred million; I heard the number of them. And thus I saw the horses in the vison: those who sat on them had breastplates of fiery red, hyacinth blue, and sulfur yellow; and the heads of the horses were like the heads of lions; and out their mouths came fire, smoke and brimstone (Revelation 9:14 +).

By these PLAGUES a third of mankind were killed by the fire and smoke and brimstone, which came out of their mouths (Revelation 10:1). And I saw another mighty angel coming down from heaven, clothed with a cloud. And a rainbow was on his head, his face was like the sun, and his feet like pillars of fire. He had a little book open in his hand. And he sat his right foot on the sea and his left foot on the sand. He raised up his hand to heaven and swore by him who lives for ever and ever, who created heaven and the things that are in it, and the Earth and the things in it, and the sea and the things that are in it, that there should be delay no longer. But in the days of the sounding of the *seventh angel, when he is about to sound; the mystery of* God would be finished, as he has declared to his servants the prophets (Revelation 10:7).

And another angel followed, saying, "Babylon is fallen, is fallen, that great city, because she has made all nations drink of the wine of the wrath of her fornication." Then a third *angel* followed them, saying with a loud voice, if anyone worships the beast and his image, and receives his mark in his forehead or in his hand, "He himself shall also drink of the wine of the wrath of God, which is poured out full strength into the cup of his indignation. He shall be tormented with fire and brimstone in the presence of the holy angels and the presence of the Lamb. And the smoke of their torment ascends forever and ever; and they have no rest day or night, who worship the beast and his image, and receives the mark of his name." Revelation 14:14 continues: Then I looked, and behold, a white cloud, and on the cloud sat one like the Son of man, having on His head a golden, crown, and in His hand a sharp sickle. And another angel came out of the temple, crying with a loud voice to him that sat on the cloud. "Thrust in Your sickle and reap, for the time has come for you to reap, for the harvest of the earth is ripe." So he who sat on the cloud thrust in his sickle on the earth, and the earth was reaped. Then another *angel* came out from the altar, who had the power of fire, and he cried with a loud cry to him who had the sharp sickle, saying, Thrust in your sharp sickle and gather the clusters of the vine of the Earth, for her grapes are fully ripe, so he threw it into the great winepress of the wrath of God. And the winepress was trampled *outside the city, and blood came out of the winepress, up to the horse's bridles, for one thousand six hundred furlongs.*

One furlong equals 220 yards, times 1,600, times 3, divided by 5,280, equaling 200 miles. The wrath of God is not finished. There are seven *angels* yet to speak. … I saw another sign in heaven, great and marvelous: seven *angels* having the seven last plagues, for in them the wrath of God is complete …. And out of the temple came the seven *angels* having the seven plagues, clothed in pure bright linen, and having their chest girded with golden bands. … I heard a loud voice out of the Temple saying to the seven *Angels,* **"Go and pour out the bowls of the wrath of God on the Earth."** So the *first* went and poured out his bowl upon the Earth, and a foul and loathsome sore came upon the men which had the mark of the beast and those who worshiped his image. The *second angel* poured his bowl on the sea, and it became as the blood of a dead man; and every living creature in the sea died.

Then the *third angel* poured out his bowl on the rivers and springs of water, and they became blood. And I heard the angel of the waters saying: You are righteous, O Lord, the One who is and who was and who is to be, because you have judged these things. For they have shed the blood of saints and prophets, and you have given them blood to drink. For it is their just due. And I heard another voice from the altar saying, Even so, Lord God Almighty, true and righteous are your judgments.

Then the *fourth angel* poured out his bowl on the sun, and power was given him to scorch men with fire. And men were scorched with great heat, and they blasphemed the name of God who has power over these plagues; and they did not repent and give him glory.

Then the *fifth angel* poured out his bowl on the throne of the beast, and his kingdom became full of darkness; and they gnawed their tongues because of the pain. They blasphemed the God of Heaven because of their pains and their sores, and did not repent of their deeds.

Then the *sixth angel* poured out his bowl on the great river Euphrates, and its water was dried up, so that the way of the kings of the east might be prepared. And I saw three unclean spirits like frogs coming out of the mouth of the dragon, and the mouth of the beast and of the false prophet. For they are the spirits of demons, performing signs, which go out to the *Kings of the Earth and of the whole world, to gather them to the Battle of that day of God Almighty.* ***"Behold I am coming as a thief. Blessed is he who watches and keeps his garments, lest he walk naked and they see his shame."*** And they gathered them together to the place called in Hebrew, Armageddon. Please note that Megiddo is about 52 miles north of Jerusalem, *capital city of the Nation of Israel.* We surely remember when President Trump declared it to be their capital and ordered his state department to move the U.S. Embassy there (2020). Megiddo has historically been the **Battlefield of KINGS** (Revelation 16), *especially Israel: About 700 B.C.* The Hebrew Prophet Isaiah wrote: Come near you Nations, to and to listen you people: Let the Earth, and all that is therein; the WORLD and all things that come forth of it. For the Indignation of the LORD is upon all nations, and His Fury upon all their ARMIES. HE HAS UTTERLY DESTROYED THEM, he has delivered them to the slaughter. Their slain also shall be cast out, and their stink shall come up out of their carcasses, and the mountains shall be melted with their blood. And all the host of heaven shall be dissolved, and heavens shall be rolled together as a scroll: and all their host shall fall down, as the leaf falls from the vine, and as a falling fig from the fig tree. For *my sword* shall be bathed in heaven: behold, it shall come down upon Idumea, and the people of my curse, to judgment

The Sword of the Lord is filled with blood; it is made fat with fatness, and with the blood of lambs and goats, with the fat of the kidneys of rams: for the Lord has a sacrifice in Bozrah, and great slaughter in Idumea.

And the unicorns will come down with them, and the bullocks with the bulls, and their *land* will be soaked with blood, and their dust made fat with fatness.

For it is the ***day of the Lord's vengeance, and the year of recompenses for the CONTROVERSY OF ZION*** (Isaiah 34:8).

This is the "Day that equals seven years of TRIBULATION for planet Earth." The controversy of NATIONS (Jeremiah 25:31): KINGS exist by the will of GOD. He alone chooses KINGS at His pleasure. "Blessed be the name of God for ever and ever: for wisdom and might are his; and he changes the times and seasons: **he removes Kings and sets up Kings: he gives wisdom to the wise and knowledge to those who know understanding.** *He reveals the deep and secret things: He knows what is in the darkness and the light dwells with him*" (Daniel 2).

The Lord RULES in the kingdom of men. The great battle of Armageddon is really a series of battles that start at Megiddo AND END AT JERUSALEM. The distance is only about 52 miles. The time of these battles is within the fullness of times (Ephesians 1:10). These times begin in early times at about 640 B.C. (2 Kings 23:29). "In his days (of Josiah): Pharaoh Necho

King of Egypt went up against the King of Assyria to the river Euphrates: and King Josiah went against him and was slain by him at Megiddo when he saw him. And his servants carried him in a chariot dead from Megiddo to Jerusalem." In this case God chose to remove him from kingship by death in battle.

In the fullness of our period of time God has removed and set up many "kings" in many ways; for example, in 1963 President John Kennedy was assassinated in Dallas, Texas. Many have thought there is proof the assassin was a member of the president's motorcade and shot him from behind. All evidence was locked away in secret for fifty years. When was finally released it revealed nothing of proof. The motive for the shooting was never mentioned. But now we could make the case that John Kennedy was removed from office because as a G7 HEAD OF THE NEW WORLD ORDER, he disobeyed rulers by refusing to send U.S.A. troops to the Vietnam War. It should be of great interest to us that the first thing his vice president did was to declare war on Vietnam. Then John Kennedy's brother Bobby, the attorney general, was assassinated by a Muslim.

Then later on President Ronald Reagan (a G7 HEAD) was shot by an assassin but only wounded; God would not allow him to die from that bullet. We should also note that both presidents were confessed Christians.

ELEVEN WAR KINGS OF PLANET EARTH (Daniel 7), 600 B.C.

In the first year of Belshazzar, king of Babylon, Daniel had a dream and visions of his head upon his bed; then wrote the dream, and told the sum of the matters. Daniel spoke and said, I saw in my visions by night, and behold the four winds of heaven strove upon the Great Sea *(the Mediterranean Sea).* And four great beasts came up from the sea, diverse one from another. And the first was like a *lion,* and had eagle's wings; I beheld till the wings thereof were plucked, and it was lifted up from the earth, and made to stand upon the feet as a man, and a man's heart was given to it. (Author: *I would like to pause here and explain the true meaning of this first beast as follows; in Daniel, chapter 4, the beast is the Babylonian king Nebuchadnezzar. The two wings represent two kinds of man changed from unsaved to saved within a period of seven times: years.)* Verse 5: And behold another beast, a second, like to a bear, and it had raised up itself on one side, and it had three ribs in the mouth of it: and they said thus to it, Arise devour much flesh *(the WARS of Media Persia, which equals Iran);* After this I beheld another like a Leopard (336 B.C.), which had upon the back of it four wings as of a foul; the beast had also four heads and dominion was given to it. *(I will explain this verse; this is a description of Greece with Alexander the Great King [head] of it: Because of his WARS of conquering the known world, he died at a young age.)*

GOD'S WAY of removing him: His kingdom was divided into four parts. The next beast (100 B.C.) was ROME (the people that crucified the Lord Jesus Christ). After this I saw in the night visions, and beheld a fourth beast dreadful and terrible, and strong exceedingly; and great iron teeth: it devoured and brake in pieces, and stamped the residue with the feet of it: and it was diverse from all the beasts that were before it; and it had TEN HORNS (verse 8); I considered the horns, and, behold, there came up among them another **little horn,** before whom before whom there were three of the first horns plucked up by the roots: and behold, in this horn were eyes of man, and a mouth speaking great things. *(The Romans had an advantage of Greek mathematics and other engineering technology, which the Romans used and added to as time went on. This increased their power. Their military [IRON TEETH] power was immense.)*

There is a time break between verse 7 and verse 8: a space of 2,600 years: from Daniel to the Cross of Jesus Christ Lord and King of the Jews. That's 733 years; from the cross to World WAR II, 1941 years. To the establishment of the ten Horns (United Nations); 4 years. To the establishment of the of the G7 (Heads) of Nations within the United Nations. … Establishment of the Nation Israel *May 15, 1948.*

Franklin Roosevelt, Winston Churchill, and Joseph Stalin were heads of their United Nations, and every President of the U.S.A. from then to now has been a G7 Head. Now to Isaiah 66:7-8: "Before she travailed she brought forth; before her pain came she was delivered of a man child. Who has heard such a thing? Who has seen such things? Shall the Earth be made to bring forth in one day? Or shall a nation be born at once? For as soon as Zion *(Israel)* travailed she brought forth her children. Shall I bring to the birth, and not cause to bring forth? Saith the Lord: shall I cause to bring forth, and shut the womb? Saith thy God. Rejoice you with Jerusalem, and be glad with her all you that love her; rejoice for joy with her, all that mourn for her. Now we go to Revelation 12:1: "And there appeared a great wonder in heaven; a WOMAN *(Israel)*, clothed with the sun, and the moon under her feet and upon her head a crown of twelve stars. And she being with child cried, travailing in birth, and pained to be delivered. And there appeared another wonder in heaven; and behold a great red dragon, having ***SEVEN HEADS AND TEN HORNS, AND TEN CROWNS UPON HIS HEADS*** (written in the Bible about 95 A.D.). This establishes the **time gap** between Daniel's ten horns and the seven years of Revelation 12. Here we live at about 1,900 years plus the tribulation to follow. And it starts the **clock of Israel's time, moving again on its way to the beginning of the 70th week of Israel's AGE: which begins** *ten horns are ten kings' kingdoms, which makes up the commercial area of trade (BABYLON THE GREAT). This system **is here with us in a modified high-tech form. BUT it is still INCOMPLETE! The known world is waiting for this person called the Little Horn here in that time; in our time he is called the ANTICHRIST, and unbelieving mankind will accept him as their Messiah.***

Israel's troubles are continued through the tribulation as Israel is carried into great WARS. And she (the woman, Revelation 12:2), being with child, cried, travailing in birth, and pained to be delivered. … And the woman brought forth a man child, who was to rule all the nations with a rod of iron: and her child was caught unto God, and to his throne. And the woman fled into the wilderness where she has a place prepared of God, that they should feed her there for 2,260 days.

WAR IN HEAVEN (Revelation 12:7)

WAR in Heaven: Michael and his angels fought against the dragon; and the dragon fought and his angels. And he prevailed not; neither was their place found any more in heaven. And the great dragon was cast out, that old serpent, called the Devil and Satan, which deceives the whole world: he was cast out into the earth, and his angels were cast out with him. ... And I heard a loud voice saying in Heaven, now is come salvation and strength, and the kingdom of our God, and the power of his Christ; for the accuser of our brethren is cast down which accused them before our God day and night.

And they overcame him by the blood of the Lamb, and by the word of their testimony; and they loved not their lives unto death. Therefore rejoice you heavens, you that dwell in them. Woe to the inhabiters of the Earth and of the sea! For the Devil is come down to you, having great wrath, because he knows he has but a short time.

And when the dragon saw that he was cast into the Earth, he persecuted the woman which had brought forth the man child. And to the woman were given two wings of a great eagle, that she might fly into the wilderness, into her place, where she is nourished for a time, and times, and half a time from the face of the serpent. And the serpent cast out of his mouth water (PEOPLE) as a flood THAT HE MIGHT CAUSE HER TO BE CARRIED AWAY BY THE FLOOD. Now we stop here in Revelation and go to the book of Ezekiel Chapter 38, and show the *continuation* of the FLOOD of the serpent; where it is confirmed in Revelation 12:15:

And the word of the Lord came to me, saying, Son of man set your face against Gog, the land of Magog, the chief prince of Meshech and Tubal: and prophesy against him. And say, Thus sayeth the Lord God; Behold I am against you, O Gog, the chief prince of Meshech and Tubal:

And I will turn you back, and put hooks into your jaws, and I will bring you forth, and all thine army, horses and horse-men, all of them clothed with all sorts of amour, even a great company with bucklers and shields, all of them handling swords:

Persia (IRAN), Ethiopia, Libya with them; all of them with shield and helmet:

Gomer and all his bands; the house of Togarmah of the north quarters, and all his bands: and many people with thee. Be thou prepared, and prepare for yourself, you and all your company that are assembled with you and you be a guard unto them.

After many days you shall be visited: In the latter years you shall come into the land that is brought back from the sword, and is gathered out of many people, against the mountains of Israel, which have always been waste: but it is brought forth out of the nations, and they shall dwell safely all of them.

You shall ascend and come like a storm, you shall be like a cloud to cover the whole land, you and all your bands, and many people with you.

Thus says the Lord God; it shall also come to pass, that at the same time shall things shall come into your mind. And you will think an evil thought: And you will say, I will go up to the land of unwalled villages; I will go to them that will be at rest, that dwell safely, dwelling without walls, and having neither bars nor gates.

To take a spoil, and to take a prey; to turn your hand upon the desolate places that are now inhabited, and upon the people that are gather out of the nations, which have gotten cattle and goods, that dwell in the midst of the land.

Sheba, and Dedan, and the merchants of Tarshish, with all the young lions, shall say to you, Are you come to take a spoil? Have you gathered your company to take a prey? To carry away silver and gold, to take away cattle and goods, to take a great spoil? Therefore:

Son of man prophesies and says unto Gog, Thus saith the Lord God; In that day when my people of Israel dwells safely, shall you not know it? (*Please note, as I write this I heard the prime minister say [on the net], "Israel must have two things to exist: the right to exist and the POWER TO KEEP IT."*)

And you shall come from your place out of the north parts, you, and many people with you all of them riding upon horses, a great company, and a mighty army:

And you will come up against people of Israel. As cloud to cover the land; it shall be in the latter days, and I will bring you against my land, that the nations may know me, when I shall be hallowed in thee, O Gog, before their eyes.

Thus says the Lord God; are you he of whom I have spoken in old time by my servants the prophets of Israel, who prophesied in those days for many years, that I would bring you against them?

And it shall come to pass at the same time when Gog shall come against the land of Israel, says the Lord God, that my fury shall come surely, up in my face. For in my jealousy and in the fire of my wrath have I spoken in that day there shall be a great shaking in the land of Israel;

So that the fishes of the sea, and the fowls of the heaven, and the beasts of the field, and all creeping things that creep on the Earth, and all the men that are on the face of the Earth, shall hake at my presence, and the mountains shall be thrown down, and the steep places shall fall, and every wall shall fall to the ground.

And I will call for a sword against him though out all my mountains, says the Lord God; every man's sword shall be against his brother.

And I will plead against him with pestilence and with blood; and I will rain upon him, and upon his

bands, and upon the many people that are with him, an overflowing rain and great hailstones, fire, and brimstone.

Thus will I magnify myself; and I will sanctify myself; and I will be known in the eyes of many nations, and they shall know that I am the Lord.

THESE WORDS by the Prophet were written 2,800 years ago, and they describe the WAR that has not yet happened of the Antichrist against Israel. And they tell us with perfect description of the Nation of Israel now (2020). They have transformed a poor deserted place into a beautiful Garden of WEALTH! They have developed the most advanced technology: the envy of the world. Surrounded by nations that hate them, they have discovered vast wealth of oil and gas, chemicals, purified water, exports of agricultural produce, and even Technology. All of this has happened in the last seventy-two years.

This prophesy in Ezekiel is confirmed by the Hebrew Christian Apostle John: written in the New Testament about 95 A.D. It is continued in Revelation 12:14: And to the woman (Israel) were given two wings of a great eagle (a Boeing 737?), that she might fly into the wilderness, into her place, where she is nourished for a time, and times, and half a time, from the face of the serpent. And the serpent cast out of his mouth water as a flood after the woman, that he might cause her to be carried away of the flood. And the Earth helped the woman, and the Earth opened her mouth, and swallowed up the flood *(of people)* which the dragon cast out of his mouth. And the dragon was angry with the woman, and went to make WAR with the remnant of her seed, who keep the commandments of God and have the testimony of Jesus Christ. *Note: The continuation and finish of this WAR is described in Ezekiel 39: "Therefore, thou son of man, prophesy against Gog, and say thus says the Lord God; Behold I am against thee, O Gog the chief prince of Meshech and Tubal: and I will turn you back and leave but the sixth part of thee …. And Thou shall fall upon the mountains of Israel, thou and all thy bands, and the people that are with you." Now back to Revelation 14:*

It is wonderful to know this is testimony of the **ANGEL flying in the midst of heaven, having the *Everlasting Gospel to preach to THOSE WHO DWELL ON EARTH, and* to every nation, and kindred, and tongue, and people, Saying, with a loud voice, Fear God, and give glory to him; for the hour of his judgment is come: worship him that made heaven**

and the Earth, and the sea, and the fountains of waters ….

And I stood upon the sea, and I saw a beast rise up out of the sea, having seven heads and ten horns, and upon his heads ten crowns and upon his heads the name of blasphemy. And the beast which I saw was like a leopard, and his feet were as the feet of a bear, and his mouth as the mouth of a lion; and the dragon gave him his power, and his throne, and great authority. And I saw one of his *heads* as it were wounded to death; and his deadly wound was healed: and all the world wondered after the beast.

And they *worshipped the dragon, which gave power to the beast: and they worshipped the beast (Antichrist), saying, who is like unto the beast? Who is able to make WAR with him?* And there was given to him a mouth speaking things and blasphemies; and power was given to him to continue forty-two months. And he opened his mouth in blasphemy against God, to blaspheme his name, and his tabernacle, and those who dwell in heaven.

And it was given to him to make WAR with the saints, and to overcome them; and power was given him over all kindreds, and tongues, and nations ….

And all that dwell on the Earth shall worship him, *whose names are not written in the book of life of the Lamb slain from the foundation of the world. If any man have an ear let him hear.*

He who leads into captivity shall go into captivity: He who kills with the sword must be killed with the sword. Here is the patience and the faith of the saints. We have seen the WAR against the woman Israel: Now we examine the Antichrist's WAR against the two witnesses of God.

And there was given me a reed like a rod: and the *Angel* stood, saying, Rise and measure the Temple of God, and the altar and those who worship therein, but the court which is without the Temple leave out, and measure it not; for it is given to the gentiles: and the holy city shall they tread under foot forty and two months.

And I will give power to my two witnesses, and they will prophesy one thousand, two hundred and sixty days, clothed in sackcloth.

These are the two olive trees and the two candlesticks standing before the Lord of the whole Earth. And if any man will hurt them, fire will proceed out of their mouth and devour their enemies: and if any man will hurt them, he must in this manner be killed.

These have power to heaven that it rain not in the days of their prophesy: and have power over the waters to turn them to blood, and to smite the Earth with all plagues, as often as they will. And when they shall have finished their testimony, the beast that that ***ascends out of the bottomless pit shall make WAR with them, and shall overcome them, and kill them!*** THE BEAST OUT OF THE BOTTOMLESS PIT IS THE ANTICHRIST. (The bottomless pit is Satan's Prison! I must stop here and explain this incredible scene. These two men are like no other in the history of mankind. Remember what we have seen takes place in modern **JERUSALEM, in a time of seven years of tribulation yet the future.** Who are they and where did they come from? We get the answer from the Hebrew prophet Zechariah 4:1 [B.C. 500]):

"And the ***Angel that talked with me came again, and waked me, as a man that is wakened out of his sleep, and said to me, what do you see? And I said, I have looked, and behold a candlestick all of gold, with a bowl on the top of it, and his seven lamps thereon, and seven pipes to the seven lamps, which are on the top thereof: And two olive trees by it, one upon the***

right side of the bowl, and the other upon the left side thereof." Note: The Hebrew Christian Apostle wrote in Revelation 11:3-4 in the year A.D. 95, "And I will give power to my two witnesses. And they will prophesy one thousand, two hundred and sixty days." We can confirm this by the writing of the Apostle Paul (who was educated in Hebrew Law, in the household of King Herod). And Paul saw the resurrected Christ on his way to Damascus. At that time, he was appointed to be an Apostle of Jesus Christ. In the following years, he wrote several books of the New Testament. In his book of Romans 11:13-29 he wrote, "For I speak to you Gentiles, inasmuch as I am the Apostle of the Gentiles, I magnify my office: if by any means I may provoke to jealousy those which are my flesh (the Jews), and might save some of them."

For if the casting away of them be the reconciling of the world, what shall be the receiving of them be, but life from the dead? For if the first fruits be holy, the lump is also holy: and if the root be holy, so are the branches. And if some of the branches broken off and you being a WILD olive tree, were grafted *in among them, and with them partake of the root and fatness of the olive tree; boast not against the branches. But if you boast, you bear not the root, but the root thee.* You will say then, the branches were broken off, that I might be grafted in.

Well: Because of unbelief they were broken off, and you stand by faith. Be not high minded but fear: for if God spared not the natural branches, take heed that he also spare not thee.

Behold therefore the goodness and the severity of God: on them who fell away, severity, but toward thee goodness if you continue in his goodness: otherwise you also shall be cut off. And they also, if they abide not still in unbelief shall be grafted in: for God is able to graft them in again:

For you were cut out of the olive tree which is wild by nature, and were grafted contrary to nature into a good olive tree: How much more shall these which be grafted into their own olive tree? For I would not, brethren, should you be ignorant of this *Mystery*, lest you be wise in your own conceits: that blindness in part is happened to Israel, until the fullness of the gentiles be come in. [We must remember that Israel was grafted into their own land in 1948 from the nations of the world to their OWN LAND.]

And so all Israel shall be saved: as it is written, "There shall come out of Sion the Deliverer, and shall turn away ungodliness from Jacob …. Israel is (as we speak) one of the most powerful nations on Earth. So it is easy to see that all the words of all the prophets have been fulfilled. In addition to that concerning Israel God shows us how he delivers them SPIRITUALLY: back to Revelation 11 and Zechariah 4, we know that the two olive trees are *types of* Israel and the church, for they are the two witnesses of God upon this Earth. Note: The two men who preach the Gospel are acknowledged in Revelation 11:4: The two Olive Trees are two flesh-and-blood men, different from all other men. They are ENOCH — he pleased God and God took him to stand by Him (Genesis 5:24, at least 6,000 years ago; still alive until in the tribulation) — and ELIJAH — God took him to heaven with his Chariot of fire (2 Kings 2:11, at least 4,500 years ago; still alive).

We prove this to settle all argument: by Hebrews 9:27, *"And it is appointed unto MEN ONCE TO DIE, BUT AFTER THIS THE JUDGMENT.* Their deaths are accomplished by the Beast (Antichrist), who makes **WAR** with them in Jerusalem, the Capital of ISRAEL: and kills them. They are made to lie on the street of the great city, which spiritually is called Sodom and Egypt, where also our Lord was crucified.

And they of the people and kindreds and tongues and nations shall see their dead bodies three days and a half and shall not allow their dead bodies to be put in graves. And they that dwell upon the Earth shall rejoice (in 2020 who does NOT dwell on the Earth? *Air men on space platforms!!)* over them, and make merry, and shall send gifts one to another; because these two prophets tormented them that dwelt on Earth. And after three days and a half, the spirit of life from God entered into them, and they stood upon their feet; and great fear fell upon them which saw them, and the same hour was a great earthquake, and the tenth part of the city fell, and in the earthquake were slain of men seven thousand: and the remnant were frightened, and gave glory to the God of Heaven. The second WOE is past, and behold, the third woe comes quickly. And the seventh *Angel* sounded: and there were great voices in heaven saying,

The kingdoms of this world are become ***the kingdoms of our Lord and of his Christ: and he shall reign for ever and ever.***

Now we come to the mystery of the fourteen tribes of Israel: forgotten and *remembered in Revelation 7:3.*

Jacob's (Israel's) twelve sons, when Israel was in Egypt, were being used as slaves. God sent Moses to deliver

*them. Israel's son Joseph had become the ruler in Egypt, second only to Pharaoh. Joseph (which means adding) and an EGYPTIAN woman, had two sons, MANASSEH and Ephraim. These two tribes with the other TWELVE TRIBES are REARRANGED to show **the passage of time from the first Tabernacle in Numbers 2, all the way to destruction of the first Temple, the Cross of Jesus Christ, King of the Jews, and to destruction of Herod's temple, then destruction of Jerusalem AND dispersion of the nation into all the world.***

The Pictures translate the Hebrew names into their meaning in ENGLISH. **ALL PICTURES GLORIFY JESUS OF NAZARETH, KING OF THE JEWS:**

FIRST PICTURE: Numbers 2 (B.C. 4000)

NORTH

Genesis 45:1-9, 49:1-33

Banner: EAGLE Message: The righteous

DAN Judge delights in his good

ASHER Words, mercy, and truth

NAPHTHTALI

WEST EAST

Banner: MAN LION Banner, Song of

Solomon 2:4

Ephraim JUDAH

Manasseh ISSACHAR

BENJAMIN ZEBULON

Message: The most Praise the King
Blessed man bears having borne our
Double fruit on the burden, brings to his
On the right hand dwelling: Reward
of power TABERNACLE
OF WITNESS
SOUTH
OX CALF Banner
REUBEN
SIMEON
GAD
Message: The Son hearing
the multitude gave
Himself for our sins

SECOND PICTURE:
Revelation 7+14 (A.D.95) GOD THE FATHER
SIMEON (Hearing multitudes) **JUDAH** (Praise) (*the*)
LEVI (Joined) (with his) **REUBEN** (Son he overcame)
ISSACHAR (Reward) **GAD** (a Troop, John 18:6)

THE LAMB ON MOUNT SION Revelation 14:1
WITH HIM 144,000

ZABULON (Dwelling) **ASER** (my Happiness) (is)
JOSEPH (Adding) (the) **NEPTHALIM** (Wrestling
Ephesians 6:12)
BENJAMIN (Son of Power) **MANASSES** (Causing to forget)

Ephraim left out: Dan (judge); a judge is not needed. Revelation 14:5: "And I looked, and, lo, a Lamb stood on Mount Sion, and with him a hundred and a 144,000 having his Father's name written in their foreheads. And I heard a voice from heaven, as the voice of many waters, and the voice of a great thunder: and I heard the voice of harpers harping with their harps; And they sung as it were a new song before the throne, and before the four living creatures, and the elders; and no man could learn that song but the hundred and forty and four thousand, which were redeemed from the Earth. These are they which were not defiled with women; for they are virgins. These are they which follow the Lamb wherever he goes. These were redeemed from among men, being the first fruits unto God and the Lamb. And in their mouth was found no guile: for they are without fault before the throne of God" (Romans 11:16).

The events that follow this ANNOUNCMENT FROM HEAVEN, happen in the seven years of tribulation when the beast (Antichrist, not yet revealed) is pictured as coming from the SEA and begins in Revelation 6 and 13: Following him, another Beast comes up out of the Earth; and he had two horns LIKE a Lamb, and he spoke as a dragon. And he exercises all the power of the first beast (Antichrist) before him and causes the Earth and those who dwell in it to worship the first beast whose deadly wound was healed, and did live. (The second beast is the false prophet.)

He does great wonders so that he makes fire come down from heaven on the Earth in the sight of men and deceived them that dwell on the Earth by means of those miracles which he had to do in the sight of the beast; saying to them that dwell on the Earth that they should make an image (statue) to the beast which had the wound by a sword, and did live. (Destroying statues has become popular in the U.S.A. in 2020.) And he had power to give breath to the image of the beast, that the image of the beast should both speak and cause that as many as would not worship the image of the beast should be killed. And he causes all, both small and great, rich and poor, free and bond, to receive a mark in their right hand, or in their foreheads: And that no man might buy or sell, except he that had the mark, or the name of the beast, or the number of his name. Here is wisdom; let him that has wisdom calculate the number of the beast: for it is the number of a man; and his number is 666.

WARS OF THE LORD'S VENGENCE (part 2): Revelation 17:1:

There came to me one of the seven *angels* which had the seven vials, and talked with me, and saying unto me, Come here and I will show unto you the judgment of the great whore that sits upon many waters. With whom the kings of the Earth have committed fornication, and the inhabitants of the Earth have been made drunk with the wine of her fornication. So he carried me away in the spirit into the wilderness, and I saw a woman sit upon a scarlet-colored beast full of names of blasphemy, having seven heads and ten horns. And the woman was arrayed in purple and scarlet color and decked with gold and precious stones and pearls, having a golden cup in her hand full of abominations and filthiness of her fornication (Revelation 17+). And upon her forehead was a name written.

MYSTERY, BABYLON THE GREAT, THE MOTHER OF HARLOTS AND ABOMINATIONS OF THE EARTH. (There are twenty-seven mysteries listed in the scriptures.) And I saw the woman drunken with the blood of the saints, and with the martyrs of Jesus: and when I saw her, I wondered, seeing her with **great wonder. And the *Angel* said to me, why have you wondered?** I will tell you the mystery of the woman, and of the beast that carries her, and has seven heads and ten horns. **The beast you saw was, and is not; and shall *ascend* out of the bottomless pit. And go into destruction.** (NOTE: The bottomless pit is another name for a prison: It is the place where kings go, and Satan is the king over them: who is the *Angel of the bottomless pit where* Satan is imprisoned for 1000 years.)

And they that dwell on the Earth shall wonder, whose names were not written in the book of life from the foundation of the world, when they behold the beast that was, and is not, and yet is. And here is the mind that has wisdom. The seven heads are seven mountains on which the woman sits. (Governments are the mountains; Isaiah 2:2, "And it shall come to pass *in the last days*, that the mountain of the Lord's house shall be established on top of the mountains, and shall exalted above the hills; and *all nations shall flow in to it*. And many people shall go and say, come you and let us go up to the mountain of the Lord, to the house of the God of Jacob; and *he will teach us of his ways, and we will walk in his paths: for out of Zion shall go forth the law, and the word of the law from Jerusalem*. And he shall judge among the nations, and shall rebuke many people: and they shall beat their swords into plows and their spears

into pruning hooks: nation shall not lift sword against nation, neither shall they learn *WAR any more)* (back to Revelation 17:7-10).

The beast comes out of the bottomless pit (to rule Earth for seven years) and the beast that was, and is not, even he is the eighth, and is of the seven, and goes into destruction. And the ten horns which you saw are ten kings. Which have received no kingdom as yet; but receive power as kings one hour (seven years), with the beast. These kings have one mind, and shall give their power and strength unto the beast. (This is where the Antichrist [head of the nations] gets his power of rule.)

These shall make WAR with the Lamb, and the Lamb shall overcome them: for He is Lord of Lords and King of kings: they that are with him are called, and chosen, and faithful. And he said to me, the waters which you saw where the whore sits are peoples, and multitudes, and nations, and tongues. And the ten horns which you saw upon the beast, these shall hate the whore, and shall make her desolate and naked, and shall eat her flesh, and burn her with fire. For God has put in their hearts to fulfil his will, and to agree, and give their kingdom unto the beast, until the words of God shall be fulfilled. And the woman

which you saw is that great city which reigns over the kings of the Earth.

Revelation (chapter 18+): And after these things I saw another *Angel* come down from heaven, having great power; and the Earth was lightened with his glory. And he cried with a strong voice, saying Babylon the great is fallen, is fallen and is become the habitation of devils, and the hold of every foul spirit, and a cage of every unclean and hateful bird. For all nations have drunk of the wine of the wrath of her fornication, and the kings of the Earth, who have committed fornication with her and the *merchants of the Earth are become rich through the abundance of her delicacies.* And I heard another voice from heaven, saying,

Come out of her, my people, that you be not partakers of her sins, and that you receive not of her plagues. For her sins have reached unto heaven, and God has remembered her iniquities. Reward her as she has rewarded you, and double unto her double according to her works: in the cup which she has filled fill to her double. How much she has glorified herself, and lived deliciously, so much torment and sorrow give her: for she says in her heart, I sit a queen, and am no widow, and shall see no sorrow. Therefore shall her plagues come in one day, death, and mourning, and famine; and she shall be utterly burned with fire: for strong is the Lord God who judges her.

And the kings of the Earth, who have committed fornication and lived deliciously with her, shall bewail her, and lament for her, when they shall see the smoke of her burning, standing far off for the fear of her torment, saying, Alas, alas, that great city Babylon, that mighty city! For in one hour is your judgment come. And the merchants of the Earth shall weep and mourn over her; for no one buys their merchandise any more: The merchandise of gold and silver, and precious stones, and of pearls, and of fine linen, and purple, and silk, and scarlet, and all fragrant wood, all manner of vessels of ivory, and all manner of vessels of most precious wood, and of brass, and iron, and marble, and cinnamon, and odors, and ointments, and frankincense, and wine, and oil and fine flour, and wheat, and beasts, and sheep, and horses, and chariots, and slaves and souls of men .... As many as trade by sea, stood far off, and cried when they saw the smoke of their burning, saying, What city is like this great city ... for your merchants were the great men of the Earth; for by your sorceries (pharmakeia, which means drugs/

poisoner) were *all nations deceived.* **And in her was found the blood of prophets, and of saints, and of all that were slain upon the Earth.**

And after these things I heard a great voice of many people in heaven, saying, Alleluia; salvation, and glory, and honor, and power, belong to the Lord our God. For true and righteous are his judgments: for he has judged the great whore, which did corrupt the Earth with her fornication, and has avenged the blood of his servants at her hand ... (Revelation 19+).

I must interrupt to report President Trump's announcement (Aug. 14, 2020) that he and the Prime Minister of Israel have just signed a peace treaty with ONE of the UNITED ARAB EMERATES, seven Caliphates (kings/kingdoms). The other six are holding back. President Trump said that if he is elected in November, he will have the full treaty signed within thirty days! This is possible because of the statement of Jesus in Matthew 24:21: "And this gospel *of the Kingdom: the one He preached,* will be preached in all the world for a witness to all nations, and then, shall the END (of Israel's age) come.

That age is very close to coming upon our world. The age is seventy years, according to Daniel the prophet, as

God tells us about our time as follows: "Seventy weeks, of sevens (which equals 490 years), are determined upon thy people (Israel); and upon the holy city, to finish the transgression, and to make an end of sins, and to make reconciliation for iniquity, and to bring in everlasting righteousness, and to seal up the vision and prophesy, and to anoint the most holy. Know therefore and understand, that from the commandment to build Jerusalem to Messiah the Prince shall be seven weeks and sixty-two weeks; the street will be built again, and the wall even in troublesome times. And after sixty-two weeks Messiah will be cut off (with a Roman spear: as in Zechariah 11:10) and I took my staff, even Beauty, and cut it asunder, that I might break my covenant which I had made with all the people. And it was broken in that day: so that the poor of the flock that waited for me knew that it was the word of the Lord."

Therefore 70 weeks minus 62 weeks minus 483 years to the cross of Jesus Christ, King of the Jews. That leaves seven years which have not started yet. But it will, according to Matthew 24:21: "For then shall be Great Tribulation such as was not since the beginning of the world to this time, no, nor ever shall be. And except those days should be shortened, but for the elect's sake those days shall be shortened.

Then: if anyone says to you Lo, here is Christ, or there, believe it not for there shall arise false Christs, and false prophets, and shall show great signs and wonders; insomuch that if it were possible they shall deceive the very elect. (For many years these false prophets have been claiming to be the real Christ. But time itself has always proved them wrong.) Therefore He describes his coming in detail, for as the lightning comes out of the east and shines even to the west, so shall the coming of the Son of man be. For wherever the case is, there will the eagles be gathered together:

Immediately after the tribulation of those days shall the sun be darkened, and the moon shall not give her light, and *the stars shall fall from heaven, and the powers of the heavens shall be shaken; and there shall appear the sign of the Son of man in heaven: and then shall all the tribes of the Earth* **mourn, and they shall see the Son of man coming in the clouds of heaven with power and great glory.** And he shall send his *angels* with a great sound of a trumpet, and they shall **gather** together his **elect** from the four winds, from one end of heaven to the other (Matthew 24:29-31). We must consider this message very carefully. It tells us the TMES of His coming for ISRAEL'S AGE ONLY, not any details of his church. This is called the **Second**

Coming of our Lord. And it is called the second GATHERING. He comes to his kingdom on Earth **with** His *elect, and they include three groups of people: number one, the 144,000 Tribes of Israel; number two, their tribulation converts; number three, all Israel* (Romans 11:26).

The Gathering **for His Church** from his cross until we meet Him in the air is called "*our gathering together to HIM*" (2 Thessalonians 1:7). This gathering happens *seven years before **His second coming with His church**.* In that time period, Revelation 19+ describes the following:

And after these things I heard a great voice of a multitude of people in heaven saying, Alleluia: the salvation and the glory and the power of our God: for true and righteous are his judgments; for he has judged the great harlot which corrupted the Earth with her fornication, and has avenged the blood of his servants at her hand. And again they said Alleluia. And her smoke rose up for ever and ever. And the twenty-four elders and the four living creatures fell down and worshipped God that sat on the throne, saying, Amen; alleluia. And a voice came out of the throne, saying Praise our God, all his servants and you that fear him, both small and great. And I heard as it were the voice of a great multitude, and as the voice of many waters, and as the voice of mighty thunderings, saying, Alleluia: for the Lord God omnipotent reigns.

Let us be glad and rejoice. And give honor to him: for the marriage of the Lamb is come, and his wife has made herself ready. And to her it was granted that she should be arrayed in fine linen, clean and white: for the fine linen is the righteousness of saints. And he said to me, Write, Blessed are they which are called to the marriage supper of the Lamb. And he said to me, these are the true sayings of God. And I fell at his feet to worship him. And he said to me, See you do it not; I am your fellow servant, and of thy brethren that have the testimony of Jesus: worship God: for the testimony of Jesus is the spirit of prophecy.

And I saw heaven opened, and behold a white horse; and he that sat upon him was called Faithful and True, and in righteousness he does judge and make WAR. His eyes were as a flame of fire, and on his head were many crowns; and he had a name written, that no man knew but himself. And he was clothed with a garment dipped in blood and his name is called the Word of God. And the armies which were in heaven followed him upon white horses, clothed in fine linen white and clean. And out of his mouth goes a sharp sword, that with it he may smite the nations: And he shall rule them with a rod of iron: and he treads the winepress of the fierceness of the wrath of Almighty God. And he had on his vesture and on his thigh a name written: **KING OF KINGS AND LORD OF LORDS.** And I saw an *angel* standing in the sun; and he cried with a loud voice, saying to all the fowls that fly in the midst of heaven, Come and gather yourselves to the supper of the great God: That you might eat the flesh of *KINGS* and captains, and the flesh of mighty men, and the flesh of horses, and of them that sit on them, and the flesh of all men, both free and bond, both small and great.

And I saw the beast, and the **kings of the Earth and their armies, gathered together to make WAR against him that sat on the horse, and against his army. And the beast was taken and with him the false prophet. …**

The precise details of this last WAR are given by the Hebrew prophet Zechariah and written 2,500 years ago, and he describes that *future technology we use worldwide today: Zachariah 12:*

The burden of the word of the Lord for Israel, saith the Lord, which stretches out the heavens, and lays the foundation of the Earth, and forms the spirit of man within him. Behold I will make Jerusalem a cup of trembling to all the people round about, when they shall be in the siege both against Judah and against Jerusalem. And in that day will I make Jerusalem a burdensome stone for all people: all that burden themselves with it shall be cut in pieces, though all the people of the Earth be gathered together against it. …

In that day shall the Lord defend the inhabitants of Jerusalem; and he that is feeble among them at that day shall be as David; and the house of David shall be as God, as the **Angel of the Lord** *before* them. And it shall come to pass in that day, that I will seek to destroy all nations that come against them. And I will pour upon the house of David, and upon the inhabitants of Jerusalem, the spirit of grace and supplications: and they shall look upon me whom they have pierced, and they shall mourn for him, as one mourns for his only son, and shall be in bitterness for him, as one is in bitterness for his firstborn. In that day shall there be a great mourning in Jerusalem, as the mourning of Ha-dad-rim-mon in the valley of Me-gid-don. And the land shall mourn, every family apart; the family of the house of David apart, and their wives apart; and the family of the house of Nathan (a son of David) apart, and their wives apart; the family of the house of Levi apart, and their wives apart; the family of Shimei apart, and their wives apart.

In that day there shall be a fountain opened to the house of David and to the inhabitants of Jerusalem for sin and uncleanness. And it shall come to pass in that day, says the Lord of hosts, that I will cut off the names of the idols out of the land. And it shall come to pass, in that day, that when any shall yet prophesy, then his father and his mother that begat him shall say to him, You shall not live; for you speak lies in the name of the Lord; and his father and his mother that begat him shall thrust him through when he prophesies ….

One shall say to HIM, what are these wounds in your hands? Then he shall answer, Those with which I was wounded in the house of my friends. Awake O sword, against my shepherd, and against the man that is my fellow, says the Lord of hosts: smite the shepherd, and the sheep shall be scattered: and I will turn my hand upon the little ones. And it shall come to pass, that in all the land, says the Lord, two parts therein shall be cut off and die; but the third shall be left therein. And I will bring the third part through the fire, and will refine them as silver is refined, and will try them as gold is tried: they shall call on my name, and I will hear them: and I will say, it is my people: and they shall say, The Lord is my God.

BEHOLD, the day of the Lord comes, and your spoil shall be divided in the midst of you. For I will gather **all nations** against Jerusalem to battle; and city shall be taken, and the houses rifled, and the women ravished; and half of the city shall go forth into captivity, and the residue of the people shall not be cut off from the city. Then shall the Lord go forth and fight against those nations, as when he fought in the day of battle. **And his feet shall stand in that day upon the Mount of Olives, which is before Jerusalem on the east, and the Mount of Olives** shall cleave in the midst thereof toward the east and toward the west, and there shall be a great valley; and half of the mountain shall remove toward the north, and half of it toward the south. And you shall flee to the valley of the mountains; for the valley of the mountains shall reach unto Azal: yes you shall flee, like as you fled from the earthquake in the days of Uzziah king of Judah and *the Lord my God shall come, and all the saints with thee.*

And it will come to pass in that day, that the light shall not be clear nor dark: but it shall be one day which shall be known to the Lord, not day nor night: but it shall come to pass, that at evening time it shall be light. And it shall be in that day that living waters shall go out from Jerusalem; half of them toward the eastern sea, and half of them toward the western sea: in summer and in winter shall it be. **And the Lord shall be King over all the Earth: in that day there shall be one Lord and his name one.** And all the land shall be turned up as a plain from Geba to Rimmon south of Jerusalem: and it shall be lifted up and inhabited in her place, from Benjamin's gate unto the place of the first gate. Unto the corner gate, and from the tower of Hananeel unto the King's winepresses.

And men shall dwell in it, and there shall no more be utter destruction: but Jerusalem shall be safely inhabited. And this shall be the plague wherewith the Lord will smite the people that fought against Jerusalem; *their flesh shall consume away while they stand upon their feet,* and *their eyes shall consume away in their holes, and their tongues shall consume away in their mouth.* And it shall come to pass in that day that a great tumult from the Lord shall be among them; and they lay everyone on the hand of their neighbor, and his hand shall rise up against the hand of his neighbor. And Judah shall fight at Jerusalem; and the wealth of all the heathen round about shall be gathered together, gold, and silver, and apparel, in great abundance. And so shall be the plague of the horse, of the camel, and of the donkey, and of all the beasts that shall be in these tents as this plague. And it shall come to pass that everyone that is left of the nations which came against Jerusalem shall even go up year to year to worship the King, the Lord of hosts, and to keep the feast of tabernacles. And it shall be that who will not come up of all the families of all the earth to Jerusalem to worship the King, the Lord of hosts, even upon them will be no rain. And if the family of Egypt go not up, and come not, that have no rain; there shall be the plague, wherewith the Lord will smite the heathen that come not up to keep the feast of tabernacles. This shall be the punishment of Egypt, and the punishment of all nations that come not up to keep the feast of tabernacles.

In that day shall be upon the bells of the horses, **HOLINESS UNTO THE LORD**; and the pots in the Lord's house shall be like the bowls before the altar. Yes every pot in Jerusalem and in Judah shall be holiness unto the Lord of hosts: and all they that sacrifice shall come and take them, and cook in them. In that day there shall be no more the Canaanite in the house of the Lord of hosts.

This is the consummation of the AGE of Israel (Matthew 24:3, 13, 30).

That final seventh year the disciples asked, And he sat upon the Mount of Olives, the disciples came to him privately, saying, Tell us, when shall these things be? And what shall be sign of thy coming, and the *completion* of the age (of Israel)? It is possible that he could have answered their question in **Acts 1:6**: "When they therefore were come together, they asked him, saying, Lord will you at *this time* restore again the kingdom to Israel? And he said to them, it is not for you to know the times or seasons which the Father has put in His own power, but you shall receive power after that the Holy Spirit has come upon you: and you shall be witnesses unto me both in Jerusalem, and in all Judaea, and in Samaria, and to the uttermost part of the Earth. And when he had spoken these things, while they beheld, he was taken up; and a *cloud* received him out of their sight. And while they looked steadfastly toward heaven as he went up, behold two men stood by him in white apparel; which also said, You men of Galilee, why do you stand here gazing into heaven? This same Jesus which is taken up from you into heaven, shall so **come in like manner** as you have seen him go into heaven ….

Then they returned to Jerusalem. He will return in clouds for His Own.

SECOND COMING OF THE LORD JESUS CHRIST

This great event has been a mystery for many centuries. But we have been given much grace by the Savior who loved us and gave himself for us. In his giving he gave us special privilege. When our Lord Jesus began his ministry on Earth, he made it a teaching work of the truth that was started by God when he delivered his people from Egypt. Moses was a deliverer first and a teacher next by the special command of God.

In Exodus 3:1+, it states, Now Moses kept the flock of Jethro his father-in-law, the priest of Midian: and he led the flock to the backside of the desert, and came to the mountain of God, even to Horeb. And the *Angel* of the Lord appeared unto him in a flame of fire out of the midst of a bush: and he looked, and behold the bush burned with fire, and the bush was not consumed. And Moses said, I will now turn aside, and see this great sight, why the bush was not burnt. And when the Lord saw that he turned aside to see, God called unto him out of the midst of the bush and said, Moses, Moses, and he said, Here am I. And he said, draw not near here: put your shoes from off your feet, for the place where you are standing is holy ground. Moreover he said, I am the God of thy father, the God of Abraham, the God of Isaac, and the God of Jacob. And Moses hid his face; for he was afraid to look upon God …. And the Lord said I have seen the affliction of my people which are in Egypt, and have heard their cry by reason of their taskmasters; for I know their sorrows. … Come now therefore, and I will send you to Pharaoh, that you may bring forth my people the children of Israel out of Egypt. And Moses said unto God, who am I that I should go to Pharaoh, and that I should bring forth the children of Israel out of Egypt?

And He said, *Certainly I will be with thee. … And Moses said unto the Lord, O my lord, I am not eloquent, neither heretofore, nor since thou has spoken to thy servant: but I am slow of speech, and of a slow tongue.* And the Lord said unto him, Who has made man's mouth? or who makes the dumb, or the deaf, or the seeing or the blind? Have not I the Lord? Now therefore go, and I will be with thy mouth, and **teach you** what you will say (4:12). And you shall **teach** them ordinances and laws, and shall show them the way wherein they must walk, and the work they must do (18:20).

This shows us the importance of our understanding God's Word of Truth. **God *himself teaches His children his truth*.**

God will teach us with His KEY OF KNOWLEDGE (Luke 11:52).

This key and the rules for using it is attached in later chapters. For time's sake now we can see an important application of the key (Daniel 2:1+). And in the second year of the reign of Nebuchadnezzar he dreamed dreams, and his spirit was troubled, and his sleep went from him. And the king commanded to call the scribes, and the magicians, and the sorcerers, Chaldeans, to show the king his dreams; and they came and stood before the king. And the king said unto them, I have dreamed a dream, and my spirit is troubled to know the dream. (Paraphrased, "Tell us the dream and we will show the interpretation.) The king answered and said, the dream is gone from me, if you do not make the dream known to me, you shall be cut in pieces. ... They called Daniel and he prayed to the Lord for understanding. God answered his prayer; and Daniel rejoiced and said, ... Blessed be the name of God forever and ever; for wisdom and might are His. And it is he that changes the times and seasons; he removes kings, and sets up kings: *He gives wisdom to the wise, and knowledge to them that know understanding: he reveals the deep and secret things; he knows what is in the darkness, and the light dwells with him.* This promise of God to his disciples (and us) is shown to us in the New Testament, "**It is given to you to know the mysteries of the kingdom of heaven**" **(Matthew 13:11).**

Now we can use the **key of knowledge (Luke 11:52)** to understand the times and seasons of Israel and the church. The following is revealed to us by the Lord Jesus. In him are hidden all the treasures of wisdom and knowledge. This wisdom is from our Lord, from Colossians 2:3 and Revelation 1:1:

The Revelation of Jesus Christ, which **God gave unto him**, to show unto **his servants** things which must shortly come to pass; and he sent and signified it by his servant John: who bear record of the word of God, and of the testimony of Jesus Christ, and of all things he saw. Remember Luke 11:52, then Luke 24:25-32 and 45.

The rules when applying the keys are as follows: [1], O fools and slow of heart to believe **ALL** that the prophets have spoken: Ought not Christ to have suffered these things, and to enter into his glory? And beginning at Moses and all the prophets [2], **he** expounded unto them in ALL the scriptures *the things concerning Himself*. And they drew near to the village, where they went: and he made as though he would have gone further. But they constrained him, saying, Abide with us, for it is toward evening, and the evening is far spent. And it came to pass, as he sat at meat with him, he took bread, and blessed it, and break and gave to them. And their eyes were opened, and they knew them; and he vanished out of their sight. And they said one to another, did not our heart burn within us, while he talked with us by the way, and while [3] *HE OPENED to us the scriptures?* ... (verse 32): And he said unto them, These are the words which I spoke unto you, while I was yet with you, that all things must be, which were written in the law of Moses, and in the prophets, and in the Psalms (Old Testament): [4] *concerning me.* [5] Then *He opened their understanding that they might understand the scriptures* (verse 45). The next rule (so important) is in 2 Timothy 2:15, Study to show thyself approved unto God, a workman that needs not to be ashamed, [6] *rightly dividing the word of truth* .... Therefore: All scripture is given by God. And is profitable for doctrine, for reproof, for correction, for instruction in righteousness: That the man of God may be perfect, thoroughly furnished unto all good works (3:16-17).

Rule 6, the dividing, refers specifically to the element of TIME, which must be considered in our understanding especially in the prophecy: for example, Ephesians 1:10 tells us, "That in the **dispensation of the fullness of times** he might gather together in one all things in Christ, both which are in heaven, and which are on Earth; even in him." There are many time(s) that must be recognized and understood: Because their chronology must be properly placed. We are warned in 2 Peter 1:20, "Knowing this first, that no scripture is of any private interpretation. For the prophesy came not in old time by the *will of man*: but holy men of God spoke as they were moved by the Holy Spirit." Then in 2 Peter 3:10-18, "But the Day of the Lord will come as a thief in the night; in which the heavens will pass away with a great noise, and the elements shall melt with fervent heat, the Earth also and the works therein shall be burned up. Seeing then that all these things shall be dissolved, what manner of persons ought you to be in all holy conversation and godliness, looking for and hasting unto the coming of the day of God. Nevertheless we, according to his promise look for, new heavens and a new earth, wherein dwells righteousness ... Paul also according to the wisdom given to him …. (verse 16). As also in all his epistles, speaking in them of these things, in which are some things hard to be understood, which they that are unlearned and unstable wrest as they do also the other scriptures unto their own destruction. You therefore, beloved, seeing you know these things before, beware lest you also, being led away with the error of the wicked, fall from your own steadfastness: but *grow in grace, and in the knowledge of our Lord Jesus Christ. To him be glory both now and forever. Amen.*

Now we return to Revelation 1:1, where we have seen John receiving the command to write the words he was hearing and send them to the seven churches. Verse 10 states, "He (John) was in the spirit on the Lord's day, and I heard behind me a great voice as of a trumpet, saying, this DAY is the seven years of tribulation which is also completion of Israel's age. Saying, I am Alpha and Omega, the first and the last: and what you see write in a book, and send it to the seven churches which are in Asia; unto Ephesus, and to Smyrna, and to Pergamos, and to Thyatira, and to Sardis, and to Philadelphia, and to Laodicea. And I turned to see the voice which spoke with me. And being turned, I saw seven golden candlesticks; and one like unto the Son of man, clothed with a garment down to the foot, and girt about the chest with a golden girdle. His head and his hairs were white like wool, as white as snow; and his eyes were as a flame of fire. And his feet like unto fine brass, as if they burned in a furnace; and his voice as the sound of many waters, he had in his hand seven stars: and out of his mouth went a sharp two-edged sword: and his countenance was as the sun shining in his strength."

We must rightly divide the word of truth. The Book of Revelation is greatly symbolic (written in signs). And rightly dividing the *times,* the first division we make is: When John wrote this, the date was 95 A.D., but what it pictures happened in 700 B.C. In Daniel 3:1, Nebuchadnezzar the king made an image of gold, whose height was three score cubits, and the breadth thereof six cubits: he set it up in the plain of Dura, in the province of Babylon … then he gathered all the nobles together and ordered all to fall down and worship the image (paraphrased). Three Jews, called Shadrach, Meshach, and Abednego, refused, this made the king angry; and he ordered them to be cast into the super-hot furnace … then he looked and said, I see four men walking in the midst of the fire, and they have no hurt; and the form of the fourth is like the **Son of God.**

In Revelation 1:15, "And his feet like brass as if they *burned in a furnace.*" So we have divided the time from 700 B.C. to a time 2020 A.D. to the time showing the church age, already having lasted 2,000 years, and the tribulation (Israel's Age, yet to begin). We can now see the three divisions of Revelation. From the Cross to the Gathering of the church, they are as follows: Number one (chapter 1) concerns *the things that ARE."* Number 2 (chapters 2 and 3) concerns the church dispensation. And number three (chapters 4-7) concerns *"things that must be hereafter,"* or the dispensation of tribulation from (7:1 through chapter 20) "things after this," meaning the beginning of the kingdom of David, 1,000 years.

And I saw heaven opened, and behold a white horse; and he that sat on him is called Faithful and True, and in righteousness he does judge and make WAR. His eyes were as a flame of fire, and on his head were many crowns; and he had a name written, that no man knew but he himself. And he was clothed with a vesture dipped in blood; and his name was called the Word of God. And the ARMIES that which were in heaven followed him upon white horses, clothed on fine linen white and clean. And out of his mouth goes a sharp sword, that with it he should smite the nations: and he shall rule them with a rod of iron: and he treads the winepress of the fierceness and wrath of

Almighty God. And he had on his vesture a new name written, KING OF KINGS AND LORD OF LORDS (Revelation 19:16). And I saw an *Angel* standing in the sun; and he cried with a loud voice, saying to all the fowls that fly in the midst of heaven, Come and gather yourselves together unto the supper of the great God; that you may eat the flesh of kings, and the flesh of captains, and the flesh of mighty men, and the flesh of horses, and of them that sit on them, and the flesh of all men, both free and bond, both small and great.

And I saw the beast was taken. And with him the false prophet which wrought miracles before him, with which he deceived them that had received the mark of the beast, and them that worshipped his image These were cast alive into the lake of fire burning with brimstone. And the remnant were slain with the sword of him that sat upon the horse, which sword that proceeded out of his mouth: all the fowls were filled with their flesh. And he laid hold on the dragon that old serpent, which is the Devil, and Satan. And bound him a thousand years, and cast him into the bottomless pit, and shut him up, and set a seal upon him, that he should deceive the nations no more, till the thousand years should be fulfilled: and then he must be loosed a little season.

And I saw thrones, and they sat upon them, and judgment was given to them: and I saw the souls that were beheaded for the witness of Jesus, and for the word of God, and which had not worshipped the beast neither his image, neither had received his mark upon their foreheads, or in their hands; and they lived and reigned with Christ a thousand years. But the rest of the dead lived not again until the thousand years were finished. This is the first (foremost) resurrection: on such the second death has no power, but they shall be priests of God and of Christ and shall reign with him a thousand years. This is also **the Tabernacle of David. Jesus has the key: "And to the *angel* of the church in Philadelphia write: these things says he that is holy, he that is true, he that has the key of David, he that opens and no man shuts, and shuts and no man opens"** (Revelation 3:7).

And when a thousand years are expired, another division. Satan shall be loosed out of his prison, and shall go out to deceive the nations which are in the four quarters of the Earth, Gog and Magog, to gather them together to battle: the number of which is as the sand of the sea. And they went up on the breadth of the Earth and compassed the camp of the saints about and the beloved city: and fire came down from

God out of heaven and devoured them. And the devil that deceived them was cast into the lake of fire and brimstone, where the beast and the false prophet are, and shall be tormented day and night for ever and ever. And I saw a great white throne and him that sat on it, from whose face the Earth and the heaven fled away; and the was no place found them. And I saw the dead, small and great, stand before God; and the books were opened; and another book was opened, which is the book of life: and the dead were judged out of those things which were written in the books, according to their works. And the sea gave up the dead which were in it; and death and hell delivered up the dead which were in them: and they were judged every man according to their works.

The judgment of every human being: And **Jesus said to her (Martha),** *I am the resurrection and the life; he that believes in me, though he were dead, yet shall he live, and whomever lives and believes in me shall NEVER DIE! Do you believe this? And she said* **yes Lord I believe that you are the Christ, the Son of God, who should come into the world** (John 11:25-27).

And death and hell were cast into the lake of fire. This is the second death. And whoever was not found written in the book of life was cast into the lake of fire. **And this is the end of the last dispensation of Time.**

And I saw a new heaven and a new Earth: for the first heaven and the first Earth were passed away; and there was no more sea. And I, John, saw the holy city, new Jerusalem, coming down form God out of heaven, prepared as a bride adorned for her husband. And I heard a great voice out of heaven saying, Behold, the tabernacle of God is with men, and he will dwell with men, and he will dwell with them, and they shall be his people, and God himself shall be with them, and be their God.

And God shall wipe away all tears from their eyes; and there shall be no more death, neither sorrow, nor crying, nor crying, neither shall there be any more pain: for the former things are passed away. And he that sat upon the throne said, Behold, I (Revelation 21:5) make all things new, and he said unto me, Write: for these words are true and faithful. And he said unto me, It is done, I am Alpha and Omega. The beginning and the end. I will give unto him that is athirst of the fountain of the water of life freely. He that overcomes shall inherit all things, and *I will be his God and he shall be my son*. But the fearful, and the unbelieving, and the abominable, and the murderers, and whoremongers, and sorcerers, and idolaters, and all liars, shall have their part in the lake which burns with fire and brimstone: which is the second death.

And there come to me one of the seven *angels* which had the seven vials full of the seven last plagues, and talked with me, saying, Come here, I will show you the bride, the Lamb's wife. And he carried me away in the spirit to a great and high mountain, and showed me that great city, the holy Jerusalem, descending out of heaven from God. Having the glory of God: and her light was like unto a stone most precious, even like a jasper stone, clear as crystal; and had a wall great and high, and had twelve gates, and at the gates *twelve angels*, and names written thereon, which are the names of the twelve tribes of the children of ISRAEL, on the east:

3 GATES 3 GATES

HOLY JERUSALEM

3 GATES 3 GATES

And the wall of the city had twelve foundations, and in them the names of the twelve apostles of the Lamb. And he that talked with me had a golden reed to measure the city, and the gates thereof, and the wall thereof, And the city lies foursquare, and the length is as large as the breadth; and he measured the city with the reed, twelve thousand furlongs the length and the breadth and the height of it are equal.

(one furlong = 220 yards)

And he measured the wall thereof, an hundred and forty and four cubits, according to the measure of a man, that is as of the *angel*. And the building of the wall of it was of jasper: and the city was of pure gold like unto clear glass; and the foundations of the wall of the city were all garnished with:

ALL MANNER OF PRECIOUS STONES

And the twelve gates were twelve pearls; every several gate was of one pearl: and the street of the city was pure gold, as it were transparent glass. And I saw no temple therein: for the Lord God Almighty and the Lamb are the temple of it. And the city had no need of the sun, neither of the moon, to shine in it: for the, saved shall walk in it, and the glory of God did lighten it. And the nations of them which are saved shall walk in the light of it: and the **kings of the earth** do bring their glory and honor into it.

[Back to Rev 21:25]: And the gates of it shall not be not be shut at all by day: for there shall be no night there. And they shall bring the glory and honor of the nations into it. And there shall be in no wise enter into it anything that defiles, neither whatever works abomination, or makes a lie: but they who are written in the Lamb's book of life (22:1).

And he showed me a pure river of water of life. Clear as crystal, proceeding out of the throne of God and of the Lamb. In the midst of the street of it, and on either side of the river, there was the tree of life, which bear twelve manner of fruits, and yielded her fruit every month: the leaves of the tree were for the healing of the nations. And there shall be no more curse: but the throne of God and of the Lamb shall be in it; and his servants will serve him: and they shall see his face; and his name shall be in their foreheads. And there shall be no night there; and they need no candle, neither light of the sun; for the Lord God gives them light: and they shall reign for ever and ever. And he said to me, these sayings are faithful and true: and the Lord God of the holy prophets sent his *Angel* to show unto his servants the things which must be done.

Behold, I come quickly; blessed is he that keeps the sayings of the prophesy of this book. And I John saw these things and heard them. And when I had heard and seen I fell down to worship before the feet of the

Angle which had showed me these things. Then he said to me, see you do it not: for I am thy fellow servant, and of thy brethren the prophets, and of them which keep the sayings of this book: Worship God. And he said to me, **seal not the sayings of this prophesy of this book.** For the time is at hand. (Matthew 13:1, These sayings are to be UNDERSTOOD BY CHRISTIANS: "And the disciples came, and said unto him, why do you speak to them in parables? And he said to them, **Because it is given unto you to know the mysteries of the kingdom of heaven, but to them [non-believers], it is not given."** Almighty God *meant for his children to understand his word, that is why I attached the,* **KEY OF KNOWLEDGE, The 7 KEYS OF SCRIPTURE and THE 7 KEYS of PROPHESY** *to the later pages of this book.)* [The time really is at hand.] He that is unjust, let him be unjust still: and him which is filthy, let him be filthy still: and he that is righteous, let him be righteous still: and he that is holy, let him be holy still. And behold, I come quickly; and my reward is with me, to give every man according as his work shall be. I am Alpha and Omega, the beginning and the end, the first and the last. Blessed are they that do his commandments, that they may have right to the tree of life, and may enter in through the gates of the city. For without are dogs and sorcerers, and whoremongers, and murderers, and whoever loves and makes a lie. I Jesus have sent mine *Angel* to testify unto you these things in the churches. I am the root and the offspring of David, and the bright and morning star. And the spirit and the bride say Come. And let him that hears say. Come, and him that is athirst. Come. And whosoever will, let him take the water of life freely (Revelation 22:7+).

And if any man shall take away from the words of book of this prophecy, God shall take away his part out of the book of life, and out of the hoy city, and from the things which are written in this book. He which testifies these things saith, surely I come quickly. Amen. Even so come Lord Jesus. The Grace of our Lord Jesus Christ be with you all. Amen.

BLESSED IS HE THAT READS, AND THEY THAT HEAR THE WORDS OF THIS PROPHESY, AND KEEP THOSE THINGS WHICH ARE WRITTEN THEREIN: FOR THE TIME IS AT HAND (Revelation 1:3).

STEPS IN GROWTH OF KNOWLEDGE *and under-standing the mysteries.*

1. SINCERE MILK: I Peter 2:2 — As newborn babes DESIRE Knowledge. 2 Chronicles I:10 — "Give me now Wisdom and Knowledge: And God said

Wisdom and Knowledge is GRANTED UNTO THEE." 2 Peter 3:18 — ***But Grow in grace and in the Knowledge of our Lord Jesus Christ.***

2. HEAR HIM: Mark 9:2-7 — … and He was transfigured before them … and a cloud overshadowed them; and a voice came out of the cloud saying "this is my beloved Son … HEAR HIM." Colossians 2:2-3.

3. GOD OUR FATHER: Isaiah 28 :9 — And whom shall he teach knowledge? And to whom shall he make to understand doctrine? Those whom are weaned from the milk and drawn from the breast.

1. HOW? 1 Corinthians 1:18 — For the preaching of the cross is to them that perish foolishness; but unto us which are saved it is the power of God. For it is written, *I will destroy the wisdom of the wise, and will bring to nothing the understanding of the prudent. Where is the wise? Where is the **scribe?** Where is the disputer of this world? Hath not God made foolish the wisdom of this world? For after that … to verse 31.*

2. THE WAY: 1 Corinthians 2:7-16 — But we speak the wisdom of God in a Mystery, even the hidden

wisdom which God ordained before the world unto our glory: which none of the princes of this world knew: for had known it, they would not have crucified the Lord of glory … to verse 12; WE have *received,* not the spirit of the world, but the spirit which is of God; that we might know the things that are *freely given to us of God*. Which also we speak, not in the **words** which man's wisdom teaches, but which the Holy Spirit teaches; comparing scriptural things with scriptural … John 6:63: "The **words I speak unto you are spirit, and they are** *life*" … Deuteronomy 32:46-47: **It is** *your life* ….

The KEY of KNOWLEDGE. Part 1, LUKE 11:52-24 27-32, 44-45, Rev 1:1

Deuteronomy 32:45-47 …. His Words, Our Life

IT IS GIVEN TO YOU TO KNOW THE MYSTERIES OF THE KINGDOM OF HEAVEN

Matthew 13:11; 11:29, Philippians 3:10 = GODS POWER, Matthew 28:18, **Isaiah 28:9, Hosea 6:6**

A. *Come unto ME B. Take My Yoke (participation of Service) C. LEARN FROM ME Matthew 11:29, James 1:* **My people are gone into captivity for lack of Knowledge:**

My people are DESTROYED for lack of Knowledge; Hosea 4:6

The treasures of wisdom and knowledge are hid in our LORD JESUS CHRIST, Colossians 2:3, Job 36:22, Daniel 2:21-22, 1 Peter 2:1-2, Milk to *GROW*, 2 Peter 2:2

Our teachers are: Our Lord Jesus, Luke 24:27, Holy Spirit of GOD, John 16:13-15, GOD OUR FATHER, Isaiah 28:9 + GOD'S *approved* teachers, Jeremiah 3:15

SCRIPTURAL RULES TO APPLY THE KEY [Note John 6:63], *2 PETER 1:20, 3:16-18*

(1). THE LORD JESUS CHRIST OPENS GOD'S WORD. Luke 8:10, 24:32, 45, Revelation 1:1

We *must* LEARN FROM HIM. Psalm 94:10 Matthew 11:28-29, Luke 10:39, Daniel 2:21, 28

a. We are taught BY HIM. Ephesians 1: 17-18, 4:13-21, 1 Corinthians 2:10-11, Hebrews 11:6, 1 Chronicles 28:9, Psalm 34:10

b. HE makes known the riches of CHRIST IN US. Colossians 1:27, PROVERBS 2:6, 3:13-26

The Holy Spirit is our Comforter.

What the Spirit of Truth hears (in this world), he makes known to us by HIS words, 1 Corinthians 2:13

He will show us THINGS TO COME (in the prophetic Scriptures), John 15:13, 6:63, by HIS words

He shall GLORIFY THE LORD JESUS CHRIST (not himself)

(2). LOOK FOR THE LORD JESUS CHRIST IN ALL SCRIPTURE, Luke 24:27,44

(3). STUDY *ALL* THE SCRIPTURE, 2 Timothy 2;15

(4). BELIEVE ALL THE SCRIPTURE, Luke 24:25

STUDY (5). RIGHTLY DIVIDE The Word of Truth. 2 Timothy 2:15, Ephesians 1: 1-12 *DISPENSATIONAL TIMES*

(6). COMPARE Scripture with Scripture, 1 Corinthians 2:13, John 6:63, 2 Peter 1:20, 3:16

(7). Pray for WISDOM, James 1:5, 6 Daniel 2:21, 23, 9:4, 22-23

(8). STUDY TIMES and SEASONS, 1 Thessalonians 5:1-10, Genesis 1;14, Matthew 24:29, Daniel 2:21, Psalm 16:7

(9). STUDY TYPES, 1 Corinthians 10:1-11, Hebrews 8:5, Deuteronomy 18:15

a. Joseph Type of Christ's FIRST Appearance. Genesis 37:4, 8, 28, 41:43, 42:8, 43:26, 45:1-3, 49:22-26

b. Benjamin Type of His Third Appearance, Genesis 35:18, 49:22-26

(10). Study SHADOWS, Example: Many Old Testament Events, Objects, Worship, Feasts, and People are Shadows and Patterns of the New and Future, Hebrews 8:5, 9:23

(11). Study PARABLES, Example: the Sower, Luke 8:4-15 — The Lord uses Symbols (word pictures)

STUDY SUBJECT Rule #6 must be applied here. God's Word is called:

1. GOD John 1:1, Revelation 19:13 The WORD OF GOD

2. SPIRIT John 6:63, 1 Corinthians 2:13

3. LIFE John 1:4 1 John 1:1-2, His Words are Life

4. LIGHT 2 Corinthians 4:4, Glorious Gospel

5. LAMP Psalm 119:105

6. TRUTH John 14:6, 17:17, 2 Timothy 2:15

7. WATER John 3:5, 4:10, 14, 15:3 Ephesians 5:26,

8. SEED 1 Peter 1:23, James 1:18, Luke 8:11

9. SWORD of THE SPIRIT Ephesians 6:17

Edge 1. The New Birth 1 Peter 1:23, James 1:18, John 6:63: Cleanses us Eph 5:26:

Increases Faith Gal 3:2, 3, Romans 10:8: Divides and Discerns Heb 4:12, Ephesians 6:17

Edge 2. Destroys Revelation 2:16, 19:15, 21, Psalms 138:2, Isaiah 34:4-8

10. TWO-EDGED SWORD Hebrews 4:12

(12). *DO NOT BE SLOW TO BELIEVE THE* SCRIPTURE OF TRUTH Luke 24:25, Daniel 10:21

WORD OF FAITH Romans 10:8, James 1:18, 2 Timothy 3:16

***BEWARE OF FALSE PROPHETS* Matthew 7:15-23**

Study Dispensations of TIMES Ephesians 1:10 HIS TIMES 1 Timothy 6:15

STUDY TIMES of Daniel:

1. 8:23 The Latter Time: Appearance of the "King of fierce countenance" (The LITTLE HORN) Antichrist

When the transgressors are come to the full.

2. 2:28 What shall befall thy people (Israel) in the LATTER DAYS 11:33-35 [Israel grafted in Romans 11:23]

3. The TIME APPOINTED: a. Last end of the indignation: Isaiah 10:24-25, 26:20-21 b. Wars of Syria and Egypt

THAT IN THE DISPENSATONS OF THE FULLNESS OF TIMES Ephesians 1:10

1. INNOCENCE Genesis 2:17

2. CONSCIENCE Genesis 7:11

3. HUMAN GOVERNMENT (one government, race, economy, one money, Genesis 11:1-4, Becomes the NEW WORLD ORDER in 1950)

4. PROMISE Genesis 12:1-7

5. CHURCH Matthew 16:18

6. TRIBULATION Matthew 24:21 (29)

7. KINGDOM Revelation 20:3

SEVEN KEYS OF SCRIPTURE

1. The Key of David Isaiah 22:20-22 (740 B.C.) given to Eliakim= The God of risings (resurrections). Used by Jesus in his Letter to Philadelphia, the one he loves (95 A.D.), and to the Tabernacle of David Acts 15:16

2, 3. The Keys of the Kingdom. Matthew 16:17, used First in ACTS 2:28, Hebrew church. Second ACTS 10:34-48. Gentiles.

4. Key of the Bottomless Pit Revelation 9:1-2, 11:7, 17:18, 20:3, 20:7

5. Key of Hell Revelation 1:18 and

6. Death Revelation 20:13, Hebrews 2:9, 1 Corinthians 15:54

7. The Key of Knowledge Luke 11:52, Jeremiah 23:30 *"I AM AGAINST THE PROPHETS, SAYS THE LORD, THAT STEAL MY WORDS EVERY ONE FROM HIS NEIGHBOR."*

SEVEN KEYS OF PROPHESY

1. Daniel 2:20-23 Almighty God is the one who changes times and seasons, gives wisdom to the wise and knowledge to those who have understanding.

2. DANIEL CHAPTER 7 READ

3. DANIEL CHAPTER 8 READ

4. DANIEL 9:24: Seventy weeks are determined upon thy people, and upon thy holy city, to finish the transgression, and to make an end of sins, and to make reconciliation for iniquity, and to bring in everlasting righteousness, and to *seal up the vision and prophesy, and to anoint the most Holy.* Know therefore and understand, that from the going forth of the commandment to restore and to rebuild Jerusalem unto Messiah the prince shall be seven weeks, and three score and two weeks: the street shall be built again, and the wall even in troublesome times. And after sixty two weeks shall Messiah be cut off, but not for himself: [A.D. 33 the spear in the side of Jesus Christ as he died on the cross] and the people of the prince that shall come shall destroy the city and the sanctuary: and the end thereof shall be with a flood, and unto the end of the WAR desolations are determined. And he (the antichrist) shall confirm the covenant with *many* for one week: (of 7 years). And in the midst of the week he shall cause the sacrifice and the oblation to cease, and for the overspreading of abominations he shall make it desolate, even until the consummation, and

that determined shall be poured upon the desolate. (Matthew 24:15). A.D. 33

5. Matthew 24: 7, 8, The beginning of sorrows .... Verse 9: *then shall they deliver you up to be afflicted, and shall kill you, and you shall be HATED OF ALL NATIONS.* **(Begins the new world order's attempt to destroy Israel.)**

The beast, the Antichrist has rule Revelation Ch 6

6. Isaiah 10:5-23 and Revelation 13:1-18 calculate 666.

7. Keys in Revelation: 17:9, 12, 15, 18, 20:1, 22:10

THE SEVEN RESURRECTIONS

1. THE LORD JESUS CHRIST John 11:25, 1 Corinthians 1:23, Romans 1:4, Colossians 1:1, Revelation 1:3, 1 Peter 3:21

2. MANY SAINTS Matthew 27:52-53, Leviticus 23:16

3. JUSTIFIED SAINTS 1 Thessalonians 4:16-17

4. TWO WITNESSES Revelation 11:11-12

5. THE LIVING Daniel 12:1, Psalm 69:28, Isaiah 4:3

6. TRIBULATION SAINTS Daniel 12:2, Matthew 13: 39

7. FOREMOST RESURRECTION Revelation 20:4, 5

Raising and judging of *the unsaved* dead. Revelation 20:12-15, John 5:29

The wages of sin is death; but the gift of God is eternal life THROUGH JESUS CHRIST OUR LORD. Romans 6:23

"What must I do to be saved? BELIEVE ON THE LORD JESUS CHRIST AND YOU SHALLBE SAVED." Acts 16: 31

HOW? But as many as received HIM to them HE gave the Guarantee to become the sons of God, even them that believe on his name. John 1:12

And the Guarantee: John 10:10-28 11:25-27 6:23 6: 35-37; Acts 4:31, 5:32 GOD BLESS YOU.

THE SEVEN BLESSINGS OF REVELATION

1:3 14:13 16:15 19:19 20:6 22:14